RESPONSES

non-fiction in context

Clayton Graves
Christine McClymont
Dennis Strauss

Nelson Canada

ISBN 0-17-603065-4

Canadian Cataloguing in Publication Data

Main entry under title:
Responses: non-fiction in context three
For use in schools.
ISBN 0-17-603065-4
1. Readers (Secondary). I. Graves, Clayton. II. McClymont,
Christine. III. Strauss, Dennis, Lyle, 1937- .
PE1121.R47 1991   428.6   C90-095787-5

1 2 3 4 5 6 7 8 9 BP 96 95 94 93 92 91

Printed and bound in Canada

PROJECT DEVELOPMENT: *Joe Banel*
COORDINATING EDITOR: *Jean Stinson*
SENIOR EDITOR: *Magdalena Hernas*
EDITOR: *Katrina Preece*
RESEARCHERS: *Marjorie Hale, Eleanor Philips*
DESIGN AND ART DIRECTION: *Holly Fisher and Associates*
COVER DESIGN: *Holly Fisher*
TYPESETTER: *Nelson Canada*
PRINTER: *The Bryant Press Limited*

Acknowledgments

Illustrations

Kathryn Adams: 105, 107, 109, 111; Adam Shaheen: 70, 71; Eric Colquhoun: 57, 133, 134, 135; Sue Denti: 74, 77; Sharon Foster: 64, 65, 66, 67; Don Gauthier: 60, 61; Sue Gauthier: 89, 114, 157; Donna Gordon: 151; Laurie Lafrance: 10, 11, 13; Emmanuel Lopez: 50, 51, 52, 54; Joe Morse: 178, 179, 180, 181, 182; Tracy Walker: 17, 18, 19, 20, 22, 100, 168; Farida Zaman: 30, 31, 32.

Photos

Jeremy Jones: 6, 7, 8; CanaPress: 16; The Vancouver Sun/CanaPress: 20; Mary Evans Picture Library: 25, 26, 27, 28; Giuliano Colliva/The Image Bank: 30; Jeremy Jones: 34, 35, 36, 37; William Campbell: 39, 40; James Ho Lim: 43; The Library of the University of British Columbia: 45; Courtesy of Shu Tung Wong: 48; Mark Gerson/courtesy of Random House Inc.: 55; The Mansell Collection: 59; Art Resource: 62; CanaPress: 66; Chronicle-Herald/Len Wagg/CanaPress: 72; H. Armstrong Roberts/Miller Comstock: 75; CanaPress: 76, 78; H. Armstrong Roberts/Miller Comstock: 79; CanaPress: 83, 85; Courtesy of Amy Siamon: 88, 89, 91, 92; Raymond Gendreau: 95; Helen Thayer: 97, 98; The Mansell Collection: 101, 102; Black Cultural Centre for Nova Scotia: 101; First Light Photographers Associated: 105; Eric Hayes: 107, 108; Greg Locke/Picture Works Inc.: 109; Gary Fiegehen: 111; National Archives of Canada: 115, 116, 119; Courtesy of Random House: 121; Sherry Gerstein/courtesy of Random House: 123; Motion Picture & Television Photo Archive: 126, 127, 128; Courtesy of CTV Television Network Limited: 130; CBC Television: 129, 130; Courtesy of TG Magazine, 202 Cleveland St., Toronto, ON, M4S 2W6: 137, 138, 139 (Alistair Eagle): 141; Moe Doiron/CanaPress: 140; Courtesy of David Ikeda: 142; CanaPress: 144 (left); Globe and Mail/Jeff Wasserman/CanaPress: 144 (right); CanaPress: 145; CanaPress: 146 (left); Dave Buston/CanaPress: 146 (right); CanaPress: 147 (top left); Dieter Endlicher/CanaPress: 147 (top right); CanaPress: 147 (bottom); Mary Evans Picture Library: 153; National Archives of Canada: 158, 169; National Archives of Canada: 163, 164, 165; The Toronto Star/K. Faught: 167, 168; Courtesy of the National Gandhi Museum, New Delhi, India: 172; Photographs from the film "Gandhi," copyright ©1982 Indo-British Films, Ltd. Reprinted by permission of Newmarket Press, 18 East 48 St., New York, NY 10017: 173, 175; Lorraine C. Parow: 179; Chris Mikula/courtesy the Citizen, Ottawa, Canada: 180; CanaPress: 185; Michael Cooper/courtesy of Stratford Festival Archives: 188; Robert C. Ragsdale/courtesy of Stratford Festival Archives: 190.

Text

Permission to reprint copyright material is gratefully acknowledged. Information that will enable the publisher to rectify any error or omission will be welcomed.

"Who We Are: How Some Canadian Students Found Out" by Jessica Pegis copyright © 1990 by Nelson Canada A Division of Thomson Canada Limited. "Why Do Teens and Parents Fight?" by Nancy J. White, reprinted with permission—The Toronto Star Syndicate. Copyright © 1988 by the Toronto Star Syndicate. "Environmental Almanac" by Warner Troyer and Glenys Moss from CANADIAN GREEN CONSUMER GUIDE by Pollution Probe. Used by permission of the Canadian Publishers, McClelland and Stewart, Toronto. Copyright © 1988 by McClelland and Stewart. "Oh, to Be a Knight" by Sean Armstrong copyright © 1990 by Nelson Canada, A Division of Thomson Canada Limited. "Record Review: The Great, Late Bob Marley" by Matt Lumsdon copyright © 1990 by Nelson Canada, A Division of Thomson Canada Limited. "Beat the Street" by Margo Beggs copyright © 1990 by Nelson Canada, A Division of Thomson Canada Limited. "Healing the Ravaged Land" by Maryanne Vollers copyright © 1988 by the National Wildlife Federation. Reprinted from the January/February 1988 issue of *International Wildlife*. "A Writer's Notes: An Interview with Paul Yee" by Linda Granfield copyright © 1990 by Nelson Canada, A Division of Thomson Canada Limited. "Occupation: Cryptozoologist" ("Tracking Down Monsters") by Richard Wolkomir copyright © 1986 by the National Wildlife Federation. Reprinted from the March/April 1986 issue of *International Wildlife*. "A Writer's Notes: Fantastic Mr. Dahl" by Lauren Wolk copyright © 1990 by Nelson Canada, A Division of Thomson Canada Limited. "Hoaxed!" by Elizabeth MacLeod copyright © 1990 by Nelson Canada, A Division of Thomson Canada Limited. "Science Fiction, Science Fact" by Jennifer Li copyright © 1990 by Nelson Canada, A Division of Thomson Canada Limited. "Fabulous Fads" by Elizabeth MacLeod copyright © 1990 by Nelson Canada, A Division of Thomson Canada Limited. "Memories Are Made of This: The Fifties Teen Fashions" by Melinda McCracken from MEMORIES ARE MADE OF THIS by Melinda McCracken reprinted by permission of James Lorimer & Company Ltd., Publishers. Copyright © 1975 by Melinda McCracken. "Starting Anew in Canada" by Barry Broadfoot from THE IMMIGRANT YEARS—FROM EUROPE TO CANADA 1945-67 by Barry Broadfoot is used by permission of Douglas & McIntyre Ltd. Copyright © 1986 by Barry Broadfoot. "The Trials of Treeplanting" by Jessica Pegis copyright © 1990 by Nelson Canada, A Division of Thomson Canada Limited. "Polar Dare" by Priscilla Turner; reprinted with permission Ms. Magazine. Copyright © 1989. "Cudjoe and Nanny, Heroes of the Maroons" by Kat Mototsune copyright © 1990 by Nelson Canada, A Division of Thomson Canada Limited. KEEPERS OF THE EARTH: "Zoe Lucas: Wildlife Biologist" by Tony Leighton copyright © 1990 by Tony Leighton; "Daniel Ashini: Native Leader" by John Goddard copyright © 1990 by John Goddard; "Sarah Pugh: Student" by Heather Pringle copyright © 1990 by Heather Pringle; all three reprinted courtesy of *Equinox Magazine*, January/February 1990. "A Sublime Gamble with Death" by John Melady from PILOTS by John Melady copyright © 1989 by John Melady. Used by permission of the Canadian Publishers, McClelland and Stewart, Toronto. "A Writer's Notes: Virginia Hamilton" by Jessica Pegis copyright © 1990 by Nelson Canada, A Division of Thomson Canada Limited. "Do TV Programs Reflect Our Society?" by Susan Smith copyright © 1990 by Nelson Canada, A Division of Thomson Canada Limited. "The Story of a Story" by Alison Dickie copyright © 1990 by Nelson Canada, A Division of Thomson Canada Limited. "Careers in the Media" by Cathy Stunden-Hall copyright © 1989 TG Magazine. Reprinted courtesy TG Magazine...Voices of Today's Generation, 202 Cleveland St., Toronto, ON M4S 2W6. "Managing Editor: Maintaining a Sense of Community" by Kat Mototsune copyright © 1990 by Nelson Canada, A Division of Thomson Canada Limited. "The Mystery of the Franklin Expedition" by Elizabeth MacLeod copyright © 1990 by Nelson Canada, A Division of Thomson Canada Limited. "The School Cars of Ontario" from VOICE OF THE PIONEER by Bill McNeil. Copyright © 1988 by Bill McNeil. Published by Doubleday Canada Ltd. Reprinted by permission of Doubleday Canada Ltd. "Shanawdithit, the Last of Beothuk" by Lauren Wolk copyright © 1990 by Nelson Canada, A Division of Thomson Canada Limited. "Fond Memories of Caribou, Muskox and 'Darn Bugs'" by Leslie Mack-Mumford, reprinted with permission—The Toronto Star Syndicate. Copyright © 1988 by Leslie Mack Mumford. "The Making of *Gandhi*" (*Afterword*) by Richard Attenborough from GANDHI: A PICTORIAL BIOGRAPHY by Gerald Gold. Text copyright © 1983 by Newmarket Press. Reprinted by permission of Newmarket Press, 18 East 48 St. New York NY 10017. "Dreaming a Myth of Creation" by Jessica Pegis copyright © 1990 by Nelson Canada, A Division of Thomson Canada Limited. "How the War of the Worlds Was Waged" by Elizabeth MacLeod copyright © 1990 by Nelson Canada, A Division of Thomson Canada Limited. "So You Want to Be an Actor..." by Jeff Siamon copyright © 1990 by Nelson Canada, A Division of Thomson Canada Limited.

Contents

CHOICES

New Zealand was the first country in the world to give women the right to vote in general elections in 1893.

Vanilla, chocolate and Neapolitan are the three most popular flavours of ice cream.

It is possible to become addicted to nicotine after smoking only three cigarettes.

In 1989, Japan spent $30 billion on defence and $55 billion on pinball.

WHO WE ARE:

HOW SOME CANADIAN STUDENTS FOUND OUT

Jessica Pegis

Applewood Heights students conduct a census in the school corridors.

Have you ever noticed how often people in the news say, "And the statistics indicate that..."? Perhaps you've wondered where they got those facts, or maybe you aren't quite certain what statistics *are*. It seems as though statistics are being quoted daily—by politicians, psychologists, health and fitness experts, educators, just to name a few vocal sources!

Actually, "statistics" is just another word for information. In order to be considered a statistic, a piece of information must be collected according to certain rules that guarantee as much as possible its validity, or truthfulness. For example, if Lucy wanted to gather some information about the messiness level of the lockers belonging to students in 9C, she would be obliged to conduct her research in a fair manner. It would *not*

be fair to ask the students in 9D to comment on the lockers of 9C students; even if every single student in 9D insisted that every 9C locker resembled an alien life form, that would still not be a statistic. Lucy would have no choice but to examine the lockers herself!

A Picture of Ourselves

Since we are living in an age loaded with information, it seems natural to be curious about people who live and work next to us—their habits, tastes, likes and dislikes. That was what a group of Ontario high school students had in mind when they began collecting statistics on their school population. They started out by wanting a picture of themselves—everything from the relative neatness of lockers to how many languages students could speak. The

mini-census, known as "Applewood Today," eventually generated so much useful information that Bridget Harrison, Applewood Heights Secondary Principal, found she could even plan new courses around the results of the census. After it was discovered that fifty-nine per cent of the students in the school could speak at least two languages fluently, she decided that English courses should include authors from around the world and that the school library should expand its holdings on different nationalities.

Grade nine and ten students were involved in the first Applewood census conducted in 1989. Since that time, the school has repeated the census and involved more grades, and other schools in other Canadian communities have initiated similar projects.

Surveys and Trends

Deciding what type of information to collect was—and continues to be—one of the most interesting phases of information gathering. The original Applewood students met regularly for several weeks to come up with a list of topics, which included both the serious and the frivolous: for example, sports interests, hallway traffic patterns, racial composition of the school, teenage awareness of current events, the typical high school locker and fashion and food preferences. They also participated in a two-day seminar organized by project coordinators Bill Matthews and Doreen Johnson, where they learned about various techniques of information collection and processing.

Statistics about people are usually based on the answers they give to a series of questions. This series is known as a "survey" and may involve questions that are best answered by "yes" or "no," or so-called "open-ended" questions that allow the person being interviewed to supply an individual response. For instance, the question "Do you wear jeans to school at least twice a week?" is answered by yes or no, while "How many times a week do you wear jeans to school?" is an open-ended question. You can appreciate that, depending on the types of questions asked, the information from each team's survey would be easy or difficult to categorize as statistics. Open-ended questions yield longer, less specific answers, so that the interviewer must organize the information (also called "data") according to "trends." For example, if seven out of ten people surveyed told you their favourite food was wings with extra hot sauce, that would definitely be a trend!

Applewood Census

On Applewood Day the actual school census took place. The students had already broken up into teams—each team was organized around one topic—and had developed their questionnaires, but now the personal interviewing began. Often it meant approaching complete strangers in the hallway or cafeteria, but the teams reported that cooperation was high.

Once the interviews were completed, the students analyzed the data for approximately three weeks. Based on their painstaking research, they were

able to formulate such diverse Applewood Heights statistics as:

- Seventy per cent of the students were either not born in Canada or had one parent not born in Canada.
- Ninety per cent enjoyed going to the mall to be with their friends.
- The most popular Applewood fashions were jeans, sweat shirts, running shoes and leather jackets.

Principal Bridget Harrison says that one consequence of the census is that "it removed a lot of tension around people's different backgrounds. Our student population has changed dramatically in the last two years—there are over fifty countries represented at Applewood Heights. Before the survey, the students tended to think they were all alone or else they felt they had to be like everyone else. Now the feeling is more relaxed."

She also says that "the whole school is interested in information now. Classes are doing surveys all the time. I think it's changed the way the students see the world; they are interested in collecting and interpreting information."

The National Census

Certainly one additional benefit of the survey was that it raised the students' consciousness about the national census, which takes place every ten years. The census of 1991 coincides with the 325th anniversary of the first-ever Canadian census—a relatively small affair involving only 3 215 people! Statistics Canada hopes that as the school census idea catches on, students will be able to compare their own data with the information collected by the government. National questionnaires on housing and ethnicity, for example, may also be distributed in schools for students to adapt as needed.

It has often been said that the careers of the future will require an understanding of information technology. Whether or not the prediction comes true, learning how to gather, interpret and communicate information is an invaluable skill. When you seek or consult information—the *real* information—you don't give flimsy opinions, outrageous claims or outright prejudice a fighting chance.

And that's a decent way of measuring who everybody is.

Responding

1. Have you ever been asked to respond to a survey? What was it about?
2. What information did the students at Applewood Heights School want from their survey? How do you feel about the subjects they included in their survey? What would you have asked?
3. What difference did the survey results make to the school?

FOCUS ON RESEARCH

Conducting a Survey

1. Working with a group of students, try organizing a survey of your own. Do some brainstorming to see what you are curious about.
2. Choose a target population for a survey, perhaps the students in a particular grade in your school or common friends.
3. Make a list of the questions you could ask and edit them carefully to make sure

   - they will yield answers you can tabulate (a number, a yes or no, a series of alternatives, etc.);
   - the respondents will not notice any biases in the wording;
   - you have included a few "open-ended" questions you will scrutinize for trends.

4. Make a prediction about the results of your survey. This will make conducting the survey more interesting.
5. Survey your target population and tabulate the results.
6. Present the results to your class and interpret them, telling what conclusions your group drew from the statistics.

Extending

1. Look through a newspaper to see how much use it makes of statistical information. Can you interpret the facts given? Could you challenge any of the interpretations made by the writers or editors? Which section of the newspaper makes the most extensive use of statistical information?
2. Monitor an election campaign to study the use of surveys indicating the status of each candidate or party and the most prominent issues.
3. Arrange for a representative of an advertising firm to speak to your class about consumer research and how it affects the development and marketing of the products we buy.

WHY DO TEENS AND PARENTS FIGHT?

Nancy J. White

The stand-off lasted for three months. The mother insisted her sixteen-year-old daughter end her friendship with a girl who had dropped out of school and was doing drugs. The daughter refused. It soured their home life.

"I considered the girl a terrible influence," explains the mother. "But my daughter's answer was that I didn't have faith in her. We went on and on with it. At times I'd forget about it and let it go, but then something would trigger me and I'd be off again."

Finally the mother decided that all her harping wasn't doing any good and she dropped the subject. The daughter eventually stopped seeing the girl on her own.

"You try to keep ten steps ahead of a teenager," says the mother resignedly, "but you just have to settle for five."

Parents and teenagers have probably been at each other since time began. No doubt pubescent Cain argued with Adam and Eve.

But today's world seems so riddled with risks. Parents want to protect their kids from drugs, AIDS and alcohol. And they worry about the heated competition to get into university and land a good job. Teens, meanwhile, are pushing for more freedom, struggling to find their own identities as young adults.

"Everyone is rubbing each other the wrong way," says Diane Marshall, assistant clinical director at the Institute for Family Living in Toronto. "I tell kids they have to learn to handle their feelings in creative, not destructive, ways. And I tell parents they also have a task—to learn to separate from their kids."

One theory is that teen–parent spats are part of our evolutionary past, that they are necessary conflicts triggered by puberty to push youngsters out of the nest and start their own families.

Necessary or not, they can be traumatic. One fifteen-year-old boy has been stealing from his family. He's taken money, clothes, even the family car for joyrides. He won't go for help and he won't talk about it.

The family now keeps valuables, including pocketbooks and car keys, locked up. "There are days I feel like saying, 'You leave or I'll leave,' " says his mother. "And there are times at work I just don't want to come home. But we'll all live through it."

Trouble doesn't start simply because a youngster hits puberty, says Bernard Stein, head of adolescent psychiatry at Sunnybrook Medical Centre. He explains that although parents say things started to go bad when the child became a teenager, the personality framework was already there.

"We don't see a Jekyll-and-Hyde transformation," says Stein. "The issues are more serious so the fights are greater. The relationship between parent and child is on the same track, but more so."

In many families, adolescence is more intense than other periods, says Peter Crosby, director of program services at Huntley Youth Services. But in those families where it is, fights usually boil down to two issues: limits to what teens can and can't do, and achievements.

"Often there's this issue of underachieving," explains Crosby of the cases at the agency. "After years of getting ready for life, there's the clear expectation of doing something."

For Pam Shulman, seventeen, and her mother, Lynda Freedman, school is the touchy topic. "We fight about my marks, my interests, my initiative—all that stuff I lack," says Pam. "Mum lectures me about once a month."

She says she realizes how frustrated her mother gets with her, but she still gets angry at the lectures. "My teeth are clenched and my brain is pulsing. I'm like, 'Get away from me.'"

Freedman says she regrets that she never went to university when she was young, so she wants her daughter to have the chance. "She reminds me of me. We want to make them what we wish we were," says Freedman. "She's an ideal kid. She's just not cut out to be academic. It's not her problem, it's mine."

Teen–parent fights can sometimes be aggravated by separation or divorce. A teen angry at one parent may think he can simply move in with the other parent, so issues never get resolved, says Rhonda Freeman, director of Families in Transition.

While adjusting to a new step parent can be sticky at any age, it's especially tough with adolescents who are more verbal and more used to the way things were, adds Freeman.

Different families fight in different ways, depending on their temperaments. While some keep up a cold, steely tension, others explode with yelling and screaming.

In some, it's a war of words. "Teenagers are very good at getting you embroiled in an argument when all you meant to say was 'no,'" says one mother. "They're very talented. It seems to come naturally to them as soon as they turn thirteen."

Rather than resort to heated verbal volleys or constant carping, the experts advise negotiation, sharing some power.

"There is no easy advice, no ABCs," says Anna Crews, a family therapist. "But you do need to confirm a teenager, to believe in his trustworthiness and capacity to assume responsibility. When you don't, you have the logical consequences."

For Goody Teachman-Gerner, who has four teenagers, the key is compromise. For example, her son, who recently got his driver's licence, wanted to take the car up to the family cottage, but she didn't think he was ready for that.

Rather than fight about it, they agreed that he'll drive on out-of-town trips with her in the car to observe him. When she feels confident in his ability, he can take the car to the cottage.

"If you're reasonable, they're reasonable," says Teachman-Gerner.

Privacy is a particularly common teen battle cry. "They have to have their own space," says Diane Marshall. "Teenagers will stake their human rights on it."

At her house, the compromise was that her teenage son would clean his room once a week and not leave food in it. In return, the door would be kept shut and she wouldn't enter.

Les Fleischer, a social worker at the Adolescent Medicine Unit of the Hospital for Sick Children, says that parents need to "strike a happy medium" in setting up rules for teenagers.

"If they're not firm enough, the teens will be out of control and not feel loved," says Fleischer. "But if they're too firm the teens will rebel."

Another family counsellor tells of a teenager who was stealing from her parents. It turned out that she was angry at the very strict rules appropriate to a much younger child. When the parents eased up on her and negotiated curfews and other rules, the stealing stopped.

One father had terrible fights with a daughter after she turned fourteen. "My wife and I tiptoed around the house with our stomachs in knots," he say. "We got attacked whatever we said."

They joined the Association of Parent Support Groups in Ontario, which has self-help groups that teach parents to change their behaviour to better deal with their children.

"A year and a half ago, we couldn't sit together and have a meal, it was so tense," says the father. "Now we can sit and talk."

Tips for Family Harmony

Many people consider disagreements between teenagers and their parents inevitable in the process of children becoming adults. Whether or not this fighting is necessary, advice for eliminating it is often sought by troubled families. Many experts focus on tips for parents, assuming that the teenagers are the problem and that it is important only to the parents that family harmony be restored. But nobody likes fighting for its own sake: you want a peaceful and supportive environment as much as your parents do. While there is no one simple solution to teen–parent conflict, the following advice for teens and their parents together might help.

Earn respect. Parents should remember that teens need to feel respected. They are growing into more responsibility and should be trusted to make some choices about non-life-or-death issues. By the same token, teens should prove to their parents that they are worthy of trust and respect.

Agree on rules. Both parents and teens should be clear and consistent on rules. Rules, and their consequences if they are broken, shouldn't come as a surprise to either side.

Fight fair. Parents and teens should consult to establish fair fighting guidelines. Diane Marshall, assistant clinical director of the Institute for Family Living, suggests setting out parameters ahead of time, such as no name-calling. Dirty tactics, such as personal attacks or destruction of property, only build up resentment.

Take time-outs. Marshall also suggests postponing an argument when everyone is tired or hungry. Take a walk around the block to cool off and then return to a discussion. The important point here is to agree on cooling-off time—don't just walk away.

Be creative when dealing with some problems. Make an appointment with your parents to discuss a particular issue. Supplement verbal communication with displays to show how responsible and thoughtful you can be (if you're a teenager), or to show that you remember how difficult becoming an adult can be (if you're a parent). Take the initiative and make the other side aware of your grievances in a way that doesn't lay blame or guilt. For example, role-play a union–management strike negotiation based on the issues in a dispute. Or set up a formal debate so that each side can air its argument without interruption.

No nagging. To avoid harangues, some families place a timer on the table, limiting each side to a certain number of minutes to talk. Focusing on the main issue and avoiding emotional displays are more necessary if the clock is ticking.

Get help. If violence appears imminent, or if communication seems impossible, professional help might be needed. There are self-help groups for both teens and adults. Going outside the family for an objective viewpoint is often useful.

Although it may seem to you that your conflict with your parents and their need to control your life will go on forever, your teen years and many of the problems associated with them will eventually end. But remember that how you and your parents deal with disagreements during this period may influence the future of harmony within your family. Good luck!

Responding

Think about the feelings you experienced, the ideas that passed through your mind as you read "Why Do Teens and Parents Fight?" Which parts of the article triggered any of the following:

- a feeling of sympathy
- a sense of disbelief
- a feeling of hope
- recognition of something that has happened to you or to an acquaintance

FOCUS ON PERSONAL RESPONSE

Voicing Opinions

1. The article mentions several causes of disputes between teens and parents. What is your opinion of the importance of each cause?

   - Teen–parent spats have evolved from the basic need to push young people "out of the nest" and drive them towards independence.
   - Teen–parent disputes can be traced to mistakes by the parents made in the early stages of child-rearing.
   - Most disagreements between parents and teens are about rules and limits.
   - High expectations of parents are the basic cause of problems between teens and parents.

2. What do you think of the "Tips for Family Harmony," pages 13-14? Try ranking them according to the following scale:

   1 - Very Effective
   2 - Effective
   3 - Ineffective
   4 - Very Ineffective
   5 - No Opinion

Extending

1. Find out what agencies or organizations teens in need of help or counselling can turn to. For example, is there a Teen Hotline or similar telephone service people your age can call? Pool the information with other students in your class.
2. Write a dialogue in your journal or writer's notebook about a disagreement between a parent and a teenager.

   - Choose a problem that seems real to you.
   - Try to make the characters seem like real people.
   - Show the basic cause of the dispute if possible.
   - Apply a solution you think would work to end the dispute.

ENVIRONMENTAL ALMANAC

Recycling: the keyword in 1990s waste management.

Warner Troyer and Glenys Moss

The days when our planet seemed a safe place to live in, permanently cocooned in its ozone layer, are over. We breathe polluted air, our water is increasingly unsafe to drink. Our garbage dumps cover more and more space—and this is not to mention the waste that has traditionally been dumped in the world's oceans!

Where do we go from here, before we have made the whole world a hazardous environment for ourselves and our children?

A Canadian organization called Pollution Probe, which grew out of the University of Toronto, has made it its business to find out just what can be done to make things better here in Canada and abroad. They research industrial emissions, farming soil, consumer habits—in short, everything that could make a difference to the quality of our environment. They publish their findings in Probe Post, *a quarterly journal packed full of grim facts.*

But all is not lost. We can, and we must, educate ourselves to consume healthy produce without adding to the mountains of garbage; to protect our air, water and precious energy sources; and, of course, to educate others that success depends on cooperation of every one of us!

The following information, researched by Pollution Probe teams, covers just some areas where we can make a difference—by making the right choices.

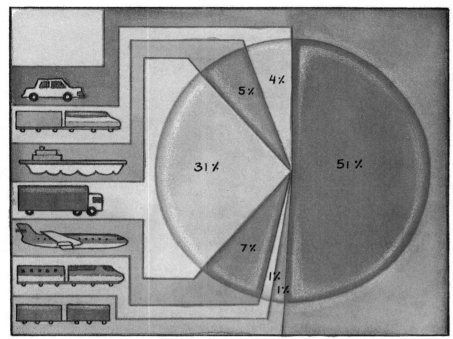

Transportation Uses of Energy (%)

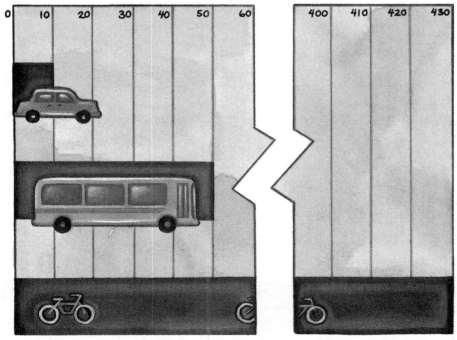

Passenger-kilometres from one litre of gas or energy equivalent

Canadians use an average of 5 000 L of water each per day; the British use 840 each and the Swiss just 350. How to account for this disproportionate consumption? Part of the answer is that most Europeans pay for their water directly via water metering.

Flat rates for water use encourage waste because they seem cheap: the rate is pitched unrealistically low while the real costs are hidden in taxes. Studies have shown that installing water meters in homes, even without rate increases, permanently reduces water use by ten to forty per cent. An example: Edmonton meters all residential water, while Calgary is only partially metered. The result? Edmontonians use half as much water as Calgarians do.

If you care about throwing too much good water down the drain, consider lobbying for municipal water metering.

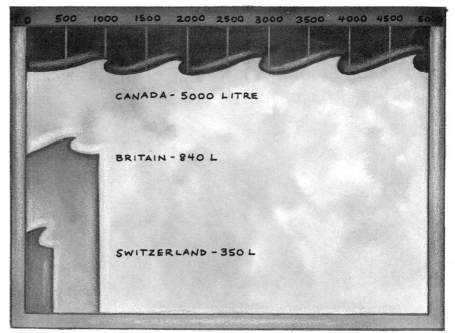

Average Daily Water Use (L)

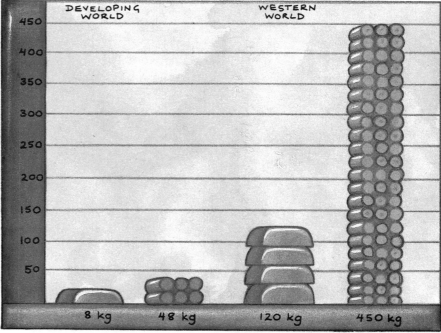

Per Capita Consumption of Paper and Steel (Kilograms)

Five Bad Packages

Until our various levels of government start to work together on reducing our packaging and hence our garbage, do your best to avoid the following examples of environment-unfriendly product wrappings.

1. Tetra-Paks: These are the square juice boxes you see in vast numbers on supermarket shelves. They can be neither reused nor recycled because they have an outer layer of plastic, a middle layer of cardboard and an inner layer of aluminum foil.

2. Blister packages: These are the cardboard-backed packages with a plastic bubble on the front to let you see the contents. Again, however, the different materials can't be separated efficiently for recycling, so they become general garbage.

3. Individually wrapped snacks: A package of cookies that has each cookie separately wrapped may seem "hygienic" at first glance, but is the second wrapping truly necessary? And do we need individually wrapped restaurant portions of butter, sugar, salt, pepper, ketchup and other condiments?

4. Single-serving microwaveables: Here too the layers of packaging are excessive. We could easily buy a larger package, take out the appropriate serving size and heat or cook it on a plate or pan.

5. Polystyrene foam egg cartons: The issue here isn't so much one of reducing packaging as it is of replacing a harmful package with a benign one. Cardboard egg cartons can be made from recycled paper, which saves resources. The foam packages can contain CFCs, which harm the ozone layer.

A cat may use up to 40 times its body weight in steel in 15 years.

Laws for the Future

1. Austria has passed a law stating that by 1992 it will be illegal to sell a package that can't be recycled. Its definition of recyclable is that there must be an operating program to collect and recycle the material.
2. Palo Alto, California, has a pilot program to label all packages with colour-coded price stickers that reflect where the product or its package will end up. Canadian cities might adopt a similar system: blue stickers on items for the Blue Box; green stickers on items for the compost bin; red stickers on hazardous household products that should go to a special depot; grey stickers on products or packages that will wind up in general garbage.
3. The state of Massachusetts is considering legislation that would put a six-per cent tax on each package. The tax would be waived entirely if the package is reusable; three cents would be waived if it's made of recycled material; and three cents would be waived if it's recyclable.

A volunteer cleans crude oil off a sea bird. Oil spillage in the open seas has become a major environmental hazard.

Shopping for a Food Store

One of the best things you can do for yourself and your family is to talk to the manager of your grocery store or supermarket about the types of food you'd like to be able to buy and the practices you'd like to see followed. Take a few minutes too to write a postcard or letter to the president or head office of each supermarket chain in your area (ask the local manager for the address). Often it takes only a few comments from concerned consumers to make retailers start thinking about changing their strategies, especially if they must do so to remain competitive. And see how many "yes" answers your store rates on the following aspects:

Bags
Does it offer a choice of different kinds?
Does it charge for bags?
Does it provide rebates for bringing your own bags?
Can bags be returned for recycling into new bags or other products?

Packaging
Does it have a meat counter where you can get products not wrapped in plastic?
Does it avoid plastic-wrapped vegetables?
Does it have a bulk section and, if so, can you bring you own containers?

Waste
Does it recycle its cardboard containers?
Does it have a recycling program in its offices?
Does it put unsold food to good use, by giving it to charities or by sending it to be composted?

Products
Does it offer certified organic food?
Does it offer alternative cleaning products in the cleaning products section?
Does it label country of origin on its produce?
Does it boycott California grapes?

Cleaning
Does it refuse to use chemical extermination techniques?
Does it use non-toxic cleaning products on its floors and fixtures?

Promotion
Does it advertise any of the above with the reason why it's important?
Does it have in-store promotional material and announcements about environmentally beneficial consumer products?

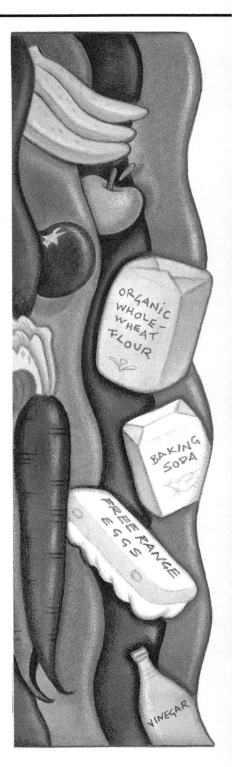

In recent years, some Canadian supermarket chains have introduced, or announced plans to introduce, products they deem "environment friendly," "natural," or "green." Of Canada's large grocery retailers, Toronto-based Loblaws has been in the forefront of producing and promoting so-called "green" items such as the Pollution Probe-endorsed President's Choice Green Baking Soda. Consumer response has been favourable, indicating there is a sizeable market for such goods. Again, environment-conscious consumers should make sure that their purchases are truly a matter of substance over style.

Ten Ways to a Greener Diet

1. Eat organic foods whenever possible, preferably Canadian ones, and don't expect perfection in appearance.
2. Where you can't find organic, try to keep your imported food choices to a minimum; off-shore pesticide controls and inspections may be less rigid than Canada's.
3. Concentrate on in-season food grown locally; out-of-season produce is shipped a long way for a long time and is often treated with chemicals to keep it from spoiling.
4. With non-organic foods, follow preparation and cooking instructions; even with organic meat and poultry you'd be wise to remove all visible fat for dietary reasons.
5. Keep yourself informed about the pesticides used on foods and the additives used in them and ask your grocer to stock foods without them.
6. Read the labels of all processed foods, on which the ingredients must be listed in order of quantity; buy the products with the fewest ingredients listed after the food itself.
7. If you're concerned about possible chemical residues or want to complain about additives in a packaged food, write to the manufacturer listed on the label; usually only the company name, city and postal code are listed, but that should be enough for a letter to reach "The President."
8. Consider sending a photocopy of your letter to the president of your grocery chain; the store manager can give you the name and address.
9. Consider, too, sending photocopies of your letter to your municipal, provincial and federal political representatives, and to the departments of health at all three levels of government.
10. Take a few minutes to write a thank-you note when you are pleased about finding an additive-free, certified organic, or otherwise environment-friendly product in a store.

Responding

1. After studying the graph on transportation uses of energy, tell what you think the distribution should be if we are concerned about energy use.
2. How would each law or program on recycling packages affect your purchasing decisions if it were in effect where you live?
3. Do you or your family commonly buy any of the "bad" packages? Could you avoid them without too much inconvenience if you wanted to?
4. Does your family have a pet which eats canned food? If so, estimate how much steel for cans it will use in its lifetime. How do your figures compare with those in the graph?
5. How do you feel about the metering of water use? Should we pay according to the amount of water we use? Why or why not?
6. Which of the suggestions for a "greener diet" sound like a good idea to you? Which ones do you follow already? Which ones would you consider following?

FOCUS ON THE READING PROCESS

Reading Graphs

The graph on page 17 tells us something about the forms of transportation we use.

- Read the caption for the graph. What information does it say the graph reveals? What do "passenger-kilometres" mean? Is this unit a measure of cost, or effectiveness or both?
- Which form of transportation yields the least number of passenger-kilometres? Which form yields the most?
- What does the graph say to city dwellers who drive to work?
- Is the graph necessarily a strong argument for travel by bicycle? What factors other than energy used must be considered?

Extending

1. Invite a panel of consumer advocates and environmental experts to speak to your class about such subjects as economical use of fuel and water, packaging and healthy diets.
2. Find out about associations and agencies which promote awareness of our environment and advocate conservation. Here are some examples:

    - Greenpeace
    - Pollution Probe
    - Environment Canada

OH, TO BE A KNIGHT

Sean Armstrong

This re-creation of a crucial time in the life of a medieval knight shows that even then young people had difficult choices to make. Someone exactly like Stephen Fitzroy may not have existed; but thousands of boys like him longed for a knight's life of battles, tournaments and courtly love.

Fifteen-year-old Stephen Fitzroy had been up since before sunrise, and he was feeling tired and hungry at the end of the day, as he unsaddled and rubbed down his horse in the stables. He had spent all day on horseback at the hunt; the riders had flushed three deer out of the densest part of the forest, and one had been shot by the young Countess; the hounds had brought it to bay by a stream, and the foresters had kept it there until the Countess rode up to take her shot.

When he finally finished tending to the horses, Stephen ran to the dining hall, led by the smell of roasting venison already strong in his nostrils. At the door of the hall, Stephen was stopped by his friend Walter. Walter was to be knighted and had spent all day at the practice of arms with the older squires. Stephen knew his friend would have bruises all over his upper body, from the blows of practice weapons.

As a squire, Walter had been preparing for knighthood for several years. His father held good lands from the Count and could support the expense of arming and equipping not only Walter, but his three brothers as well. Stephen's father had been injured in the Count's wars and his lands were too poor to pay for a warhorse and armour for his son. His father's years of service to the Count were rewarded by having Stephen live at the castle, but it was not likely Stephen would ever be made a knight. Stephen might not marry, either, and even if he did, it would be to a girl as poor and dowerless as his two young sisters.

At the table, Stephen speared a piece of meat with his hunting knife. Walter told him the news Stephen had been hearing all week: the Count had promised to send a hundred knights to help the King of Portugal—to whom he was related by marriage—in the reconquest of his kingdom. The full one hundred would be made by knighting the oldest of the Count's squires. Walter was among them.

As a new knight, Walter would now need his own squire who would look after his armour and weapons, his spare horses and all the arrangements of providing food and shelter on the road. Now, at dinner, Walter told Stephen he wanted him as his squire. Stephen was delighted—this was a great step towards someday, perhaps, achieving knighthood himself.

* * *

Some days later, Stephen began his new duties by helping Walter to prepare for the knighting ceremonies. First, Walter's hair was cut as short as a monk's. Then he was led with the other knights-to-be down to the river, to be bathed and to confess their sins. The priests led the young men back to the castle, where twenty-six straw pallets waited in the long common room. Each of the twenty-six beds had a pair of simple black wooden shoes beside it.

The shoes were to remind them of mortality, and the certainty of their eventual death; the beds were to remind them of the comforts of

At a tournament: knights in full armour crossing lances.

A joust on London Bridge in medieval England.

heaven that awaited them. In unison, Walter and the other knights-to-be recited the laws of chivalry: to obey God's teaching and defend the Church; to raise up the weak and helpless; to fight for their native land and never retreat before an enemy; to wage ceaseless war on infidels; to always obey their liege lord; and to fight for good against evil.

In the afternoon Stephen and the other squires served the young men at the last banquet of their old life. They then proceeded to the chapel, where Stephen placed Walter's weapons on the altar to be blessed, as Walter knelt with the others on the cold stone floor. The knights-to-be were locked up for the night with solemn prayers. This was the vigil, where each young man spent the night in contemplation of the life he had chosen.

* * *

In the morning, Stephen took the pale-looking Walter a cup of hot spiced wine. The castle was bustling with preparations. From mid-morning, people gathered on the lawns outside, where rich cloth was laid out on the fields and pavilions set up for the gentry. Great tables were laid for feasting and preparations were made for jousting and other martial sports that would cap the day.

Stephen stood behind Walter, holding his sword, swordbelt and a pair of spurs. An older knight faced each new knight, and as Stephen handed them over, grim old Sir Roger, best swordsman in the county, buckled Walter's sword around him, then stopped to attach the spurs. Walter waited with his head down, for now the Count himself was standing before the young men. Stephen had rarely seen the Count so close up. Walter and Stephen both knelt; then the Count took his sword—it was a famous one, sent him from Spain—to give the accolade, the tap on each shoulder that made Walter a knight. "Rise, Sir Walter, new made of my knights," said the Count.

There was a fanfare of trumpets and the crowd began cheering for the new knights and all the young squires with them. Flushed with strain and happiness, Walter put his arm around Stephen. It was time now for all the new knights to demonstrate their skills by jousting with each other and with the older, more experienced knights. Stephen ran quickly to make sure that Walter's—now Sir Walter's—warhorse and arms were ready.

The jousting took place in the lists, two runs along the length of the field, separated by a barrier of gaily painted cloth. Knights would charge at one another from each end, separated by the barrier. When they met in the middle, each knight would try to hit the other with his spear and knock him from his horse. After several runs, there would be further tests and then the knights would dismount and show their skills on foot.

Stephen helped Sir Walter into the saddle. The horse bit and stamped. Waiting where they were, behind the tents, they couldn't see what was happening. But they could hear the fanfares of trumpets, the drumming of horses' hooves and the excited shouts of the crowd. Walter kept muttering under his breath, running through the right sequence of actions again and again like a charm. Stephen fitted Walter's helmet on and laced it to the neckpiece. There was a cambric handkerchief tucked through the visor hinge—a gift to Walter from Lady Anne, one of the ladies-in-waiting to the young Countess. She was signalling that she would be his lady and perhaps in time his wife.

As Stephen waited for Walter's turn at the joust, he thought that for him there were only two ends to the road ahead: either death in the south of Portugal or a knighthood gained on the battlefield, along with the wealth to support it. A few days before, Stephen had asked a monk to write a letter to his father and sisters for him (like many of the squires, Stephen had been taught to read, but not to write), telling them he would be gone for years and might never return. There had been no time for a reply.

There was a blare of trumpets and it was Walter's turn to joust. He took his horse out into the field at a canter, as befitted a young man, while his name was announced by the herald. "Sir Walter de Lancey!" At the end of the lists, he brought his horse to a restless halt and held himself firmly in the saddle, lowering his heavy spear to the "charge" position. Another blast of trumpets and a cloth was dropped. Walter dug his knees into his horse and started down the list at a canter. At the other end, a strange knight, only his top half visible across the barrier, began to canter towards him, his spear pointing across the barrier towards Walter.

Jousting at Westminster Abbey in London, England.

Responding

1. Do you think the lives of Walter and Stephen were exciting? Why or why not?
2. What did you learn about knighthood and feudal times that you didn't know before?

Reading like a Writer

As you review the story, try to put yourself in the author's place and consider the decisions he made.

- Why do you think he wrote from the young man's perspective?
- What event did he choose as the focus of the story?
- Why did the author begin the story with Stephen, the poor boy, rather than with Walter, the squire?
- What does the author reveal about the prospects of each boy?
- What are the advantages of writing an article in story form? What limitations does the story form impose on the writer? Which do you think is superior—the story form or the article—as a means of revealing information and a form of entertainment?

Extending

1. Make a survey of the books available in your school or neighbourhood library on the subject of knighthood and read some of them. You may wish to include historical fiction in your list.
2. Get together with a group of other students and arrange to create and collect pictures and artifacts of heraldry. Consider the following ideas:

   - crests
   - coats of arms
   - sketches of knights and squires
   - a diorama of a joust
   - a scroll of the chivalric code

3. What mention is made of women in this story and what role did women play in medieval society?

Listening to the music of The English Beat, General Public and The Fine Young Cannibals, I realized it was time to pay more tribute to the influence of the late, great Bob Marley. The powerful rhythmic music that Bob Marley and the Wailers brought from Jamaican ska roots to the international concert stage in the seventies and early eighties is still growing and evolving today, providing inspiration for bands all over the world.

When reggae music started in Jamaica in the early sixties, the beat was much faster and the songs less serious than many of the best reggae songs today. But by the late sixties the beat had slowed down, the rhythm became the

THE LATE, GREAT BOB MARLEY

Dr. Spin

Bob Marley in concert. Marley's music continues to influence young musicians the world over.

A view of a Jamaican beach. It was¹in Jamaica that reggae music started in the early 1960s.

focus of the music and bass rather than guitar provided the melody.

Up until the early seventies, reggae had no widespread exposure outside the Caribbean. Many people in England had discovered ska and were dancing to its driving beat, but reggae had not yet caught on with the general public.

Then in 1972, British music entrepreneur Chris Blackwell of Island Records heard the Wailers and signed them. Blackwell had an ear for new music, as well as talent and resources necessary to bring that music to large audiences. With exposure in Britain and Europe, the Wailers quickly built a large following. Bob Marley's intelligent, heartfelt lyrics, combined with his tremendous ability to write and arrange music, began to change the future of reggae.

By the mid-seventies, Bob was beginning to influence not only the course of reggae, but almost every aspect of pop music as well. One of the first major performers to pick up on Bob's sound was Eric Clapton, who covered Marley's *I Shot the Sherriff* in 1974, one year after Bob had recorded the track. Clapton's version rose to number one in America. Soon after, Bob scored his first big hit with *Jamming,* a hot dance song which is a celebration of life and love. Stevie Wonder was so excited by *Jamming* and by Marley that he wrote *Master Blaster,* a tribute to Bob Marley and reggae.

Bob Marley was a devout believer in Rasta and much of the material that he wrote celebrates the peace and love themes central to the Rasta religion. His songs were about the beauty of nature, love and freedom. These unfaltering beliefs, combined with his great talent and worldwide influence, made him a spiritual as well as a musical leader in Jamaica. As his lyrics show, Marley was a combination superstar and revolutionary. He used his charisma and his belief in the freedom and redemption of all people to work for political change in Jamaica.

While on tour in North America in 1980, Bob Marley fell ill. The tour was cancelled and Bob was diagnosed as having cancer. Eight months later, on May 11, 1981 Bob Marley died at the age of thirty-six in a Miami hospital. His music—and his tremendous impact on other artists—lives on.

The album *Legend: The Best of Bob Marley and the Wailers* is the perfect introduction to the work of Bob Marley and the reggae roots of so many of the nineties' bands. A collection of the best and most popular of the Wailers' songs from 1972 to 1981, this broad-ranging album is a tribute to the virtuosity and versatility of a great musician.

Some of the songs show Marley's upbeat side, as does *Three Little Birds,* an uplifting celebration of the morning: three birds come to the door, singing about the peace of nature and the necessity simply to enjoy the moment. *One Love/People Get Ready* is a joyful tune reminiscent of a Gospel spiritual.

The serious, political side of Bob Marley is revealed in the song *Buffalo Soldier*. Released posthumously in 1983, this song tells the story of slaves brought from Africa to fight in the war against America's native people. Many of these Buffalo Soldiers finally escaped and settled in the Carribean and this slow, soulful, reflective song reminds Jamaicans of an important part of their history.

The collection doesn't neglect Marley's more dance-oriented hits—and includes *Stir It Up* (1973), *Jamming* (1977), and *Could You Be Loved* (1980).

The astonishing range of Marley's music is witnessed by the diversity of groups—The Police, Rush, UB40, to name but a few—which incorporate reggae's distinctive beat into their sounds. Rap tends to embrace many forms of music from blues and soul to funk and rock, and now performers like Shinehead deliver a message against drugs and violence through a mixture of rap and reggae. Many Canadian bands, such as Messenjah and The Satellites continue to develop this musical blending of styles.

Legend: The Best of Bob Marley and the Wailers is well-named. Listen to the songs that made him a legend and discover how influential he has been with musicians and listeners throughout the world.

Responding

1. Which of the following activities associated with music do you enjoy?

  - listening to recordings
  - listening to the radio
  - listening to music in public buildings
  - dancing
  - playing a musical instrument
  - singing when you're alone
  - singing with a group of friends
  - performing music for an audience

2. Make a list of the kinds of music you enjoy. What is your favourite song? Who is your favourite performer?
3. Do you enjoy reggae music? Are you a fan of Bob Marley?

FOCUS ON ORAL LANGUAGE

Technical Vocabulary

The music world has given life to many new words, changing the meanings of existing words. A glossary is a list of technical terms and their definitions, sometimes including examples and explanations. Build a glossary of the technical terms used in "Record Review: The Great, Late Bob Marley," including the following:

album	bass	lyric
Jamaican ska	music entrepreneur	rap
reggae music	exposure	funk
beat	arrange	rock
rhythm	dance song	a blend of styles

Extending

1. Get together with a partner to research the life of a favourite musician or performer. Collect information, recorded music and pictures and arrange to present a brief review to your class with the visual material as a backdrop.
2. Follow the reviews of entertainers and recording artists in magazines and your local newspaper(s). Who is your favourite reviewer? What do you like about him/her?

JUSTICE

Unit 2

Joan of Arc, who led the French against the British during the Hundred Years War, was burnt at the stake in 1431 as a witch.

In Winnipeg, it is against the law to attend a concert less than four hours after eating garlic.

Clarence Darrow was an American lawyer famous for taking the case of the underdog. He confessed late in his career that "there is no such thing as justice—in or out of court."

BEAT THE STREET

Margo Beggs

Life can be very cruel to the runaway teens who live on the streets of Toronto. For many, it may become so painful and dangerous that they turn to drugs. But is there any hope for them of getting off the street and reclaiming their lives from poverty, crime, illness and prison? Read on to find out how one Toronto organization has set out to help the city's street kids.

A tutor and his student work at a computer at the Beat the Street office in Toronto.

Two people are sitting at a table, their heads bent over a book. One is a student, the other a teacher.

"'Ro...Ro...,'" Struggles the student. Then she looks up. "I can't get it."

"You remember," says the teacher encouragingly. "It's 'Romeo.'"

"Oh yeah. 'Romeo, Romeo,'" reads the student. And with increasing confidence, "'Where...fore art thou, Romeo?'"

"Alright!" exclaims the teacher. "I knew you could do it!"

A typical exchange between student and teacher? Not quite. For one thing, they're working at a picnic table in a park. For another, they're both the same age—about nineteen. But perhaps what is most surprising is that when today's lesson is finished, these two won't pack up and go home—because they have no homes to go to. The "student" and "teacher" are both homeless teens, living on the streets of Toronto.

These particular street kids—let's call them Janet and Rob—are two of the estimated three- to five thousand kids in Toronto without permanent shelter. Day-to-day problems they must face include finding a place to sleep at night, figuring out how to pay for food and clothes—and just trying to keep safe.

With so much to worry about, why are Janet and Rob reading *Romeo and Juliet?* Because they are part of an innovative literacy program for homeless teens called "Beat the Street."

Beat the Street helps street kids get back into the mainstream of society by offering them free help with reading, writing and anything else they want to learn. The program's "teachers," or "tutors," as they are called at Beat the Street, are often volunteers who are interested in helping others find a better way of life.

People from all walks of life have been volunteer tutors with Beat the Street. The staff trains them to teach in a "learner-centred" way: to determine what the students want to learn and to figure out how to help them reach their goals. Then each tutor is matched to one student.

According to Bill Worrell, director of Toronto's Beat the Street program, "the best tutors we have are other street kids." Since the program began, the staff has pounded the pavement on "Street Walks," actively seeking out kids who want to learn—and kids who are willing to give a hand.

Director Bill Worrell: "Our goal is to help kids learn what they want to learn."

Beat the Street doesn't have any set courses. Its only goal, says Worrell, "is to help kids learn what they want to learn." While Janet sits in the park working on her high school diploma, back at the Beat the Street offices volunteers and staff help out as Ted studies a driving manual, Robin fills in a job application and Lindsay writes a letter at a computer terminal.

Beat the Street was founded in 1985 by two ex-offenders, Tracy LeQuyere and Rick Parsons. Both men had spent time living on the street, as well as in prison. But they never gave up the desire to straighten out their lives. That was tough, though, because neither man had ever learned to read or write.

It wasn't until they were in their thirties that LeQuyere and Parsons found out there were programs to help adults with reading and writing. When they discovered—in spite of what they'd been told all their lives—they could learn, they decided to help street kids get the same chance. They founded Beat the Street to spread the word that anyone can learn.

Worrell says Beat the Street tries to help participants understand that if they've had problems learning in the past, "it's not their fault. Maybe the system hasn't figured out how to teach them. Or maybe there have been other things in their lives that haven't allowed them to learn."

In the case of street kids, the odds are high that life back home got in the way of learning: a recent study on homeless kids living in Toronto reports that one-third of them ran away because of alcohol

problems in the family. That statistic is a strong reminder that most street kids aren't there because they want to be, but because life at home is even worse.

However, once you're on the street it can be tough to get off—especially if, like LeQuyere and Parsons, you can't read and write. Going on welfare isn't an option, because to get welfare you need a permanent address. To have a permanent address, you need a job so you can afford to pay rent. And for most jobs, these days, you need to be able to read and write.

When street kids are ready to break out of this Catch-22 situation, Beat the Street is there to give them another shot at learning. Co-founder LeQuyere says, "Everybody has problems. But I tell them, 'Let's not worry about yesterday, let's worry about today.'"

And he adds, with the certainty of someone who knows from experience, "If you take one step for help, that's success at its finest."

A Conversation with a "Beat the Street" Kid

"D" was living on the street in Toronto when she heard about Beat the Street. Here she talks about her experiences as a street kid.

Interviewer: *Where are you from?*

"D": A little town in Ontario.

Interviewer: *Why did you come to Toronto?*

"D": My parents were killed in a car accident. I didn't have any relatives to stay with, so I decided to come to Toronto.

Interviewer: *How did you end up on the street?*

"D": When I left for Toronto I just had enough money for a bus ticket. I arrived at the bus station with a hockey bag full of clothes, and just started staying wherever I could.

Interviewer: *What's an average day like on the streets?*

"D": A living hell. If you're a girl you have to watch out for pimps and everybody has to watch out for drugs. Most of the kids on the street are fifteen and sixteen—I'm nineteen, and *I'm* scared. The worst time is at night, when you're trying to find a place to sleep. Sometimes I slept in the subway if I didn't get kicked out. Now it's better, because I'm living in a hostel.

Interviewer: *How did you hear about Beat the Street?*

"D": From some other kids. On the street, there's sort of a community. You hear about what's going on.

Interviewer: *You've been at Beat the Street for a couple of months now. What are you getting out of it?*

"D": Since I've been going, I've grown up a lot. I'd actually finished school by the time I got to Toronto, but I've always felt I was kind of slow at reading. Beat the Street has helped me become more independent. I've found out how to do things I didn't think I could do. Now I'm thinking of going to college or university in the fall.

When I was first in the streets, I thought I'd die. Now I know I'm going to survive—and I think I'm going to make it really big some day.

Responding

1. How do you think you would feel if you couldn't read?
2. What is the aim of the Beat the Street program?
3. What is meant by teaching students in a "learner-centred" way?
4. Why do you think some students fail to learn to read? Could the schools do a better job to avert the problem? How?
5. Do you think the program's philosophy, "Let's not worry about yesterday, let's worry about today," makes sense? Why or why not?
6. If you were a taxpayer, would you like to see tax money spent on the Beat the Street program? Why or why not?

FOCUS ON RESEARCH

The Local Scene

Working with a partner, find out as much as you can about illiteracy in your community and about steps taken to help adults learn to read.

1. Identify the people who play a role in combating illiteracy.

   • Are any of teachers or officials in your school or district involved?
   • Does the local newspaper work on adult literacy through its "Newspaper in the Schools" program?
   • Are there any programs like "Beat the Street" organized in your community? Who is involved?
   • Does the government of your province sponsor a literacy program? Who leads it?

2. Think of questions to ask the personnel involved about

   • the definition of illiteracy,
   • the number of illiterate people in your area,
   • the problems illiterates face,
   • the success rate in teaching them to read and write.

Extending

1. Organize a panel presentation on literacy for the class. Include

   • one or two reading experts from your community,
   • a teacher,
   • one of the students.

   Give each panel member an angle to think of in preparing comments.
2. Interview an adult who has recently learned to read. Keep in mind that people who failed to learn to read when they were in school are understandably sensitive about the fact.

HEALING THE RAVAGED LAND

Maryanne Vollers

Before conservation came to Kanyariri, Esther Wairimu was a tree killer.

Two days each week, the Kenyan woman trudged along the red dirt paths of her village with bundles of branches lashed to her back, scouring the hillsides for firewood. Along with her other jobs of hauling water, tending crops on her husband's two-and-a-half-hectare farm and cleaning house, Wairimu had ten children to cook for over an open hearth. This required a lot of firewood. No small tree was safe.

Then in 1982, a fledgling conservation project called the Green Belt Movement arrived in Kanyariri. It began a campaign to transform Wairimu, and others like her, from tree killers into tree planters.

"My neighbours joined the Green Belt and began to argue with me," Wairimu recalls. "They said if I planted my own trees I would not have to go looking all the time for firewood." And so when the time came for Wairimu to put in her rows of maize and beans, she planted trees as well. Now, five years later, her farm is a tender woodland. Mango trees, blue gums, nitrogen-fixing casuarinas and straight-trunked podocarpus form a belt of greenery around her fields. There is shade for Wairimu's tin-roofed house, fodder for her goats and cows, better soil for her crops and branches for her firewood. "I have learned that a tree, in another way altogether, is life," says Wairimu.

The conversion of Esther Wairimu from environmental despoiler to tree planter may seem like a small victory. But it symbolizes the emerging importance of women as a powerful force for conservation. Not only are Wairimu and other rural women making strides at halting deforestation and protecting the land; women like Wangari Maathai, founder of the Green Belt Movement,

Ready for planting: Kenyan women hold seedlings just received from a Green Belt nursery.

Esther Wairimu (left) *tends her young woodland.*

are becoming leaders in the battle to solve the world's environmental problems.

The reason women are suddenly taking action is that deforestation and other environmental ills have dramatic impact on their lives. "Women bear the highest cost of the [environmental] crisis because of their role in providing water, food and energy to their families," explained a statement issued in 1985 at the United Nations' Decade for Women Conference. "Women also have the greatest potential for contributing to the solution of the crisis, precisely due to their function in the management of those resources."

And so, women around the world are taking matters into their own hands.

• In Jamaica, women started a non-polluting, solar energy salt-extraction project that brings income to rural women and offers a model solution to the country's dependence on imported salt.

• A Ghanaian women's group became fed up with a system for smoking fish that wasted huge quantities of wood and emitted harmful fumes. So the women developed a safer smoker that consumes one-tenth as much wood. The technology has spread to five other West African countries.

• Back in 1974, local women in the Himalayan region of India threw their arms around trees to stop loggers from cutting down an ash forest. The incident sparked a national environmental movement called "Chipko," or "Hug a Tree." In the 1980s, the Chipko women successfully filed suit to shut down limestone mines that were destroying hillsides.

In Kenya, where ninety per cent of the indigenous forest has been razed in the past century, the biggest and best-known project that involves women is the Green Belt Movement. Founded in 1977, the project has been responsible for the planting of nearly five million trees. Miniature forests have sprung up on school and church grounds; more than five hundred communities have their own tree nurseries, and 25 000 households like Esther Wairimu's now have thriving woodlots.

Unlike many development projects, the Green Belt does not simply open up shop in a community; it waits to be invited. Women's groups learn about it, mostly through word of mouth, and then apply to start a tree nursery. The Green Belt organization then supplies hoes and water tanks, and trains and pays a nursery attendant who is chosen by the women. The women are also taught to gather seeds from the local woodlands and to care for the seedlings. Once the young trees are given out, the Green Belt Movement pays "promoters" and "Green Belt Rangers"—usually old or handicapped people chosen by the women—to make sure the seedlings are being cared for. Because of the follow-up, about eighty per cent of the trees survive.

Responding

1. How did the Green Belt Movement change Esther Wairimu's life?
2. What do you think is the chief reason for the success of the Green Belt Movement? What arguments can you supply to defend your opinion?

FOCUS ON ORAL LANGUAGE

Informal Debate

Hold an informal classroom debate on the following topic: "The environment would be much better off if Canadians returned to the practice of backyard gardening and raising their own vegetables."

You need to do some research in order to note the effects of widespread gardening and to provide examples.

Start the debate by asking those opposed to the proposition to sit on the right side of the classroom, those in favour on the left and those undecided in the middle. As people change their views, they move to the appropriate part of the classroom. When the debate is over, it is easy to see which side has won.

Extending

1. Watch some of the television programs which deal with saving the environment, for example, *The Nature of Things*.
2. Write a proposal for dealing with an environmental problem in your area. You may wish to address the proposal to school or city officials.

   • Begin by describing the problem and its magnitude.
   • Explain who is responsible for the problem.
   • Tell what you think should be done to solve it.
   • Send the proposal to the appropriate authorities.

A WRITER'S NOTES:

AN INTERVIEW WITH PAUL YEE

Linda Granfield

Paul Yee was born in Saskatchewan and raised in Vancouver, British Columbia. He has written short stories, non-fiction and poetry in which the Canadian Chinese experience is a strong theme. His latest book Tales From Gold Mountain, *a collection of modern folktales, was awarded the Sheila A. Egoff Children's Book Prize. His book* Saltwater City *is subtitled* An Illustrated History of the Chinese in Vancouver. *Paul works as an administrator in Multicultural Records Department of the Archives of Ontario.*

Interviewer: *How did you come to write* Saltwater City?

Paul Yee: *Saltwater City* was the result of the research I did for the Vancouver 86 celebration. I worked in a centennial multi-media exhibit and planned to write a catalogue to accompany the show. An editor suggested I use the research to write a book instead. The final text is a combination of the work I did for the exhibit and my master's thesis, "Chinese Businessmen in Vancouver, 1886-1914." I ended up taking the subject matter and moving from a thesis to an academic article and then to a popular work with photos.

While I was a student at the University of British Columbia I majored in Canadian history. I worked for two summers in the City of Vancouver Archives where I began by sorting pamphlets and progressed to other jobs. After graduation I worked at the Archives for ten years. But I needed a new challenge. The Ontario Archives job was posted, I got the position and moved. I find that there is a significant difference between the Chinese communities in Vancouver and in Toronto.

Paul Yee at work: "I write systematically and in spurts and starts."

Interviewer: *What difference do you mean?*

Paul Yee: The Chinese in Toronto are primarily from the recent post-1967 immigration from Hong Kong. When I'm in Toronto people tend to assume that I am an immigrant, rather than a Canadian of Chinese ancestry. While the Hong Kong presence is strong in both cities, in Vancouver the Chinese community has a tradition that is visible in a culture entrenched over the years. The old buildings were built by the Chinese, their mark is everywhere in the community. It is a strong, visible presence that has grown over one hundred years.

At one time in British Columbia, one out of ten people was Chinese. It was easier to romanticize the Chinese community because it was in British Columbia for so long. It's not the same in Ontario. Here the focus of romanticism is the Loyalist period of history. If I had grown up in Ontario it would have been more difficult for me to find a core to write from. In Vancouver, the core, the community to which I belonged and from which I drew my stories, is part of the core of British Columbia.

Interviewer: *Was storytelling a part of your childhood in Vancouver?*

Paul Yee: My family was not a traditional storytelling family. I had an aunt who would tell bits of conversation from the past, not as narratives, but as trivia, information, bits of helpful advice, warnings and such. Some of those bits of information have come out in my stories.

In China, stories are transmitted via a number of sources. There were clapper tellers selling stories in market towns, there were travelling opera troupes and there were the classic tales of "great men and outstanding women." There were also the martial arts stories, and these came down to me via the movies and TV. These stories had a huge impact on me.

On the Western side, I had a typical dose of fables, fairy tales, legends and ghost stories that all kids growing up in urban Canada get from school and library books.

Interviewer: *Paul, your job seems to be another way for you to explore multiculturalism.*

Paul Yee: Yes. My department maintains the multicultural records of the different ethnic communities in Ontario. For instance, we have a collection of ethnic newspapers, immigrants' passports, old photographs, church records, that kind of item. Right now we're organizing the papers of a rabbi who kept a journal when he attended a war criminal's trial after World War II.

Interviewer: *What other interests have added dimensions to your writing?*

Paul Yee: Well, for five or six years I was obsessed with *taiko,* Japanese drumming. I started when I was working at the Vancouver Archives and went three times a week to practice. It is extremely physical and powerful and I *had* to do it. We made our own drums from wine barrels and stretched the skins across the tops. It is a very theatrical art form with lots of body movements. I am proud to be Asian and it is a powerful form of Asian art. In Japan, drummers are a part of the festivals; in North America, the drummers take centre stage. The power is exhilarating; fifteen drummers surrounded by motion and sound. I left the group when I realized just how much time I was devoting to *taiko.*

Writing has taken the place of drumming. I find I have more to give people with my writing. I can say more and then, in classrooms especially, I can get an intellectual and emotional response back from readers. My gift is more for writing. *Taiko* made me physically fit and in tune with my body and that has remained with me.

Interviewer: *So you've gone from an extremely physical activity to writing, where you sit for long periods of time?*

Paul Yee: (*with a chuckle*) Yes.

Interviewer: *Can you tell us a bit about how you write and what projects you're working on?*

Paul Yee: I write systematically and in spurts and starts. I map out all my chapters in an outline—I like working on more than one project at a time and the outlines make it possible to work this way. If you're writing and you get stuck on one section you can't push at it. Move on to something else.

I do all my thinking-out and writing in longhand. I never compose at the computer. An editor once asked me if the text I had given her was composed on the computer. She said that when a story is written in longhand it communicates something that is lost when the computer, not the paper, gets it first.

It takes a long time to write my stories; I rewrite a great deal. The ghost rider story in *Tales* took fourteen drafts to get right. I needed a whole new beginning for the story. That's over three years' work for a story that's only four pages long when it's printed.

I work at my kitchen- or dining room table, or outside in the nearby park or my backyard. I'm a portable writer; I jot ideas down on index cards when I'm travelling on the subway to work. I'm also very motivated by deadlines.

Right now I have a screenplay going. I was working on two short stories about my parents' experiences in Saskatoon and was thinking about a third when it suddenly became a screenplay. Sandy Wilson, who made *My American Cousin,* is involved and it's all very exciting.

I'm also working on another young adult book, a historical novel about Vancouver during the Depression. The focus will be on a father–son relationship and soccer-playing.

Interviewer: Tales from Gold Mountain *has been very successful at relating the Chinese experience in North America within the folktale tradition. Can we look forward to more tales?*

Won Alexander Cumyon, the first Canadian-born Chinese Canadian.

Paul Yee: Yes. I'm working on a sequel to *Tales.* I have about eight stories composed, but these tales will be different from those in the first book. They will examine the darker side of the human psyche. Another tale will be produced as a picture book.

Interviewer: *Your books seem to be more plot-oriented than descriptive. Why is this?*

Paul Yee: I have to confess that, for a long time, when I read, I would read dialogue only. I skipped over the parts that were heavily descriptive—wanted to know what was happening. I read mysteries as a kid, and read quickly to find out what was going on.

I see myself as a story *teller,* where the plot or storyline is most important. When you *tell* a story, the listeners can absorb only the events that are happening. The extended descriptive details of mood, setting and background work at a different level of story, I think.

I took courses in Canadian literature, as well as history in university; I didn't discover my degree was going to be in history until near the end of my university years. Most of the kids I knew in Vancouver's Chinatown studied commerce or business or medicine. Only four Canadians of Chinese ancestry were in my class in the arts faculty.

Interviewer: *How has being a member of the Chinese community in Canada influenced your writing career?*

Paul Yee: To being with, I wouldn't be a writer if I wasn't Chinese. Writing is one way to put Chinese Canadians in the mainstream of Canadian literature; it is just another part of the overall literary world. I think *Saltwater City* could have been written by a white researcher who compiled the information and reported it well. But with fiction, the author says something from within a community. I speak from inside the Vancouver Chinese community.

Non-fiction like *Saltwater City* is objective. Fiction, like *Tales,* for me is from the heart, and in my writing I try to mirror people from the heart.

Responding

1. Paul Yee says that storytelling was not part of his family tradition. How did he come to be a writer of stories?
2. What role did *taiko,* Japanese drumming, play in Yee's development as a writer?
3. Yee states that he

   • often outlines before writing,
   • works on several projects at a time,
   • drafts his ideas in longhand instead of using a computer,
   • rewrites a great deal,
   • jots ideas down wherever they come to him.

   How does his approach to writing compare with your own?
4. How does his Chinese origin affect Yee's goals as a writer?

FOCUS ON RESEARCH

The History of Your Community

Work with a partner or small group to find out as much as you can about your own local community and its history.

1. Go to any written sources such as

   • *The Canadian Encyclopedia,*
   • back issues of local newspapers (especially the year-end issues),
   • books on the origin of the names of towns and cities.

2. Brainstorm the questions remaining to be asked and divide them among the members of your group. Try to avoid questions which call for "yes" or "no" answers and concentrate on open-ended questions, such as

   • "Tell me about your earliest memories of your community."
   • "What do you recall about the sports days held in your community?"

   Use your follow-up questions to focus on further detail. From time to time, try a question with a preamble, such as news reporters use, for example, "Your community hasn't always enjoyed prosperity. Can you recall a time when its people worried about where their next meal was coming from?"

3. Arrange to interview members of your community about their memories of its development.
4. Organize the information gained into a group report and share it with your class.

Extending

Suppose you were a reporter and have just finished interviewing Paul Yee for the literary pages of your paper. Write a profile article on Paul Yee using the interview information.

• Emphasize his importance as a Canadian writer.
• Trace his work in other fields.
• Discuss his approach to writing.
• Mention his goals.

Autumn Festival celebrations in the streets of Vancouver.

STRANGER THAN FICTION

A clinical researcher in San Diego claims that children he has questioned under hypnosis were able to remember in detail their own births.

In 1704 a British sailor named Alexander Selkirk quarrelled with his captain and asked to be left on an island near Chile, where he lived alone for four years. Writer Daniel Defoe heard about Selkirk and used his story as the basis for his novel *Robinson Crusoe*.

Canadian computer scientist Alexander Dewdney created a two-dimensional fantasy planet called Astria, complete with its own laws of physics and chemistry and its own ecology.

OCCUPATION: CRYPTOZOOLOGIST

Richard Wolkomir

Despite the repeated failure of quests to track down such well-publicized beasts as the Yeti or Ogopogo, many of us are still fascinated by the news of yet another expedition on its way to the Himalayas or Okanagan Lake. What is it about us that keeps us interested in the sightings of, say, the Loch Ness Monster? And are people involved in the quests for legendary creatures wasting scarce research funds to indulge in their fantasies? This article will explore these questions and add more entries to your Bogus Bestiary.

In April 1983, a Congolese biologist slashing through unexplored central African swampland sees a large animal that resembles a species of dinosaur presumed extinct for sixty-five million years. Two months later, a University of Virginia anthropologist on New Ireland, an island near New Guinea, glimpses a marine mammal that, local residents insist, has the tail of a fish, the torso and head of a human. Meanwhile, other observers report sightings of hairy wild men in China, Sasquatches in the American Northwest, Yetis in the Himalayas and enormous octopuses in the Caribbean.

While most scientists dismiss all such reports of so-called "fabulous animals" as myths, hoaxes or at best mistakes, a small but increasingly vocal minority has been caught up in the search for the unknown. They believe it possible that species of large animals still lurk, unclassified and uncatalogued, in the world's vastnesses.

Intent on enhancing the credibility of their investigations, these unorthodox researchers have invented a name for their enthusiasm—cryptozoology, or the science of hidden animals—and have organized a society to further their investigations. They have also sparked a vigorous, sometimes bitter debate about whether they are really scientists.

The undertakings of cryptozoologists are almost always arduous, exotic, intriguing, and to romantics, disappointing. Consider, for example, a 1981 expedition to the interior of Zaire. It was co-sponsored by oilman Jack Bryant, three magazines and University of Chicago administrator and biologist Roy Mackal, who also happens to be the vice president of the International Society of Cryptozoology (ISC). Its purpose was to investigate sightings, dating back to 1776, of a beast resembling a sauropod, a herbivorous dinosaur. Zaireans call it the *Mokele-Mbembe* and report that it lives deep in the northern Congo's vast unexplored swamp.

Travelling in dugout canoes, hacking their way through the overhanging jungle with machetes, the expedition members penetrated deep into the swampy wilderness. They used sonar equipment to search the watery depths for submerged animals. Sometimes they paddled for two days at a time before finding a patch of dry land.

Once, rounding a curve in a river, the canoes pitched violently in the wake of a large animal that had just submerged. According to expedition member J. Richard Greenwell, a desert ecologist and secretary of the ISC, "our guides panicked."

The scientists took a more sanguine view. "The possibilities," as Greenwell saw it, "were hippos, elephants or crocodiles." But he knew that hippos do not

live in swamps, elephants do not submerge completely and crocodiles leave only a small wake. "It doesn't prove anything," he said, "but here was a large animal that seemingly we could not identify."

Later a Zairean hunter pointed out a wide swath through the jungle—made, he said, by a *Mokele-Mbembe*. A local government zoologist assigned to the expedition, Marcellin Agnagna, was so intrigued that he resolved to return with an expedition of his own.

He did so in April 1983. After a difficult journey, Agnagna's group reached Lake Telle, deep in the interior of the swamp. For several days they searched in vain. Then it happened.

Directly in the view of Agnagna and his colleagues, a creature surfaced. It was, Agnagna reported, "a strange animal, with a wide back, a long neck and small head." But, the scientist reported ruefully in the ISC journal, "The emotion and alarm at this sudden, unexpected event disrupted the author's attempt to film the animal."

Cryptozoologists insist that their purpose is not to confirm the existence of fabulous animals, but to investigate the possibilities. The field's founding father, French zoologist Bernard Heuvelmans, cites the eighteenth-century English novelist Oliver Goldsmith: "To believe all that has been said of the sea serpent, or the Kraken, would be credulous; to reject the possibility of their existence would be presumptuous."

Wishing to be neither credulous nor presumptuous, Heuvelmans has

In a recent issue of the scientific journal *Nature,* Princeton University zoologist Robert May wrote: "Many people feel that the correct response from scientists should be one of friendly, even encouraging tolerance. But, in truth, my reaction...is regret for the money libraries will waste on acquiring the journal and regret for the dissipated efforts that could be directed more productively to studying [tropical] species that may be going extinct at a faster rate than they are being classified."

devoted thirty-five years to cryptozoology—a term he coined in the 1950s. In 1982, he and a group of interested scientists and laymen founded the ISC to pursue, in Heuvelmans' words, "the collection, analysis, comparison, sifting out and synthesis of all available information on animals still absent from our zoological catalogues."

Heuvelmans and his colleagues like to point out that previously unknown large animals have been discovered in modern times. A large fish netted in 1938 off southern African coast turned out to be a coelacanth, thought to have been extinct for sixty million years. An entirely new species of wild cattle, the kouprey, turned up in Cambodia in the 1930s. As recently as 1976, scientists discovered near Hawaii a huge, plankton-eating shark so enormous they dubbed the creature "megamouth."

Nevertheless, critics of the discipline scoff that the study of dubious sightings, local legends and questionable fragments of evidence is not science. "These guys are claiming a gloss of respectability that isn't there," snaps one biologist. "They really are nothing more than recreational myth hunters."

Despite all such scornful and exhaustive debunking, the quest continues. Zoologist Agnagna plans to return to the search for *Mokele-Mbembe* with more and better equipment. Undoubtedly there will be new expeditions to the countries of the Sasquatch and the Yeti. Marine biologist Forrest Wood, a consultant to the U.S. Navy in San Diego, hopes to find a giant Caribbean octopus that has been reported over the years by sailors and Bahamian fishermen.

"Even when there is no animal in the hand," says oceanographer LeBlond, "there may still be one in the bush. What cryptozoology is doing is cleaning up the corners of what has not been discovered, using the classical methods of exploratory zoology."

Imagine participating in such a quest in Africa, urges anthropologist Krantz: "Then you try to convince your colleagues that you saw a creature two stories tall, with two horns on its head, each topped with a round ball, and its body covered with brown spots. They're going to stare at you in total disbelief."

Yet this bizarre creature really does exist. It's called a giraffe.

Five Monsters: Real or Not?

- **Sea Dragon:** Steaming across the South Atlantic in 1906 aboard a Dutch freighter, Captain J. Koopman was on watch one Sunday afternoon when his wheelman suddenly shouted, "Sir! Sir! Look over there." Koopman turned and saw an "enormous beast," he wrote later. "It was overtaking our ship with the speed of an arrow off a bow." It had a "monstrous head and a number of enormous dorsal fins." The captain later learned that an almost identical sighting has been made in the same area the previous year.

- **The Beast of Exmoor:** In 1983, a strange predator killed more than a hundred sheep in southwestern Britain. According to one witness, the so-called "Beast of Exmoor" "had a gleaming black coat and short powerful legs. It didn't seem to have a neck." One of the Royal Marines who were called in to hunt the killer managed to glimpse the creature, but the beast was never captured or shot.

- **A New Bear:** Villages in Nepal have long insisted that a bear other than the region's familiar black bear inhabits their forests. And so, in 1983, two American scientists went looking. In the rugged foothills of Mount Makulu, they found five nests, which appeared to be more elaborate than those of black bears, and a set of tracks going up a moss-covered cliff that was too steep for black bears to scale. In addition, they discovered three skulls. Later analysis indicated that the skulls may indeed belong to a new species.

- **Sasquatch:** The name of this giant mountain creature means "wild man" or "hairy man" in the language of the Salish. Ever since explorer David Thompson discovered huge footprints in British Columbia in 1811, images of the Sasquatch have focused not only on its size and reticence, but also on its almost human quality. In a description of a female Sasquatch given under oath in 1955, William Roe reported that, as it left, "it threw its head back and made a peculiar noise that seemed to be half laugh and half language." Sightings and evidence continue to be reported; does Sasquatch still wander the deep forests of B.C.?

- **Ogopogo:** It has been said for centuries that the depths of British Columbia's Okanagan Lake hide an enormous serpent. It has been described as anywhere from seven to twenty-five metres in length, and squadron leader Bruce Millar commented on its "dignified demeanour." Some say that, like the spelling of its name, Ogopogo appears the same viewed from either end. Disbelievers continue to discount sightings and photos as floating branches or beavers, but many still keep the belief in and fascination with Ogopogo.

Responding

1. Do you think people who practise cryptozoology are genuine scientists? Why or why not? What seems to motivate them?
2. Which, if any, of the following creatures do you believe really exists:

    Sasquatch   the Loch Ness Monster
    Ogopogo   the Beast of Exmoor
    the sea dragon   the Nepalese bear

3. Often you can tell what an unfamiliar word means by looking at its context. Find each of these words in the article, guess what it means judging by its context and look it up in a dictionary to see whether you were right.

    vastness   sparked   arduous
    exotic   intriguing   sauropod
    herbivorous   machete   wake
    sanguine   dissipated   debunking

FOCUS ON COLLABORATIVE LEARNING

A Species Study

1. Get together with a group of three or four other students to make a cryptozoological study of a strange creature such as the Sasquatch or Ogopogo.
2. Collect as much information as you can about the sightings people claim to have made, the investigations other cryptozoologists have carried out, and the scientists' reactions. Arrange the information logically to make it easier to review.
3. Brainstorm a list of criteria you will use to judge the evidence and decide whether there is real substance to the claims, for example:

    • The sighting was made by a reliable person.
    • The sighting is supported by a photo.
    • The sighting is supported by a scientific investigation.

4. Decide whether the claims are genuine and report your findings to the whole class.

Extending

1. Work together with a partner to create a strange new creature.

    • Make up a report of a "sighting."
    • Provide an "artist's recreation."
    • Give the creature a name.

A WRITER'S NOTES: FANTASTIC MR. DAHL

Lauren Wolk

Roald Dahl, the creator of such characters as Willie Wonka and Mr. and Mrs. Twit, is one of Britain's most popular writers among readers of all ages.

Roald Dahl is a man of many talents and many tastes. He knows how to fly an airplane, breed greyhounds and orchids, grow everything from onions to roses and make terrific orange marmalade. He would like to have been a good doctor, or to cure hams and salmon, or to cook eels and chicken in a small kiln and wishes that his dog could talk to him. But what he knows how to do best, likes to do best, and dreams of the most is writing.

Dahl spent his first twenty years as an author writing for adults. His books, plays, screenplays and television work won him great acclaim and earned him a fine living. But when his first child, Olivia, grew old enough for bedtime tales, Dahl turned a corner in his career. He began to create fantasies for her, stories good enough to hold the interest of a small and easily distracted child, and to turn the best of his ideas into books. "Had I not had children of my own, " says Dahl, "I would have never written books for children, nor would I have been capable of doing so." But with Olivia and, later, his other children as his audience, Dahl turned his imagination and his talents to stories that have thrilled generations. *James and the Giant Peach; Charlie and the Chocolate Factory; Danny, the Champion of the World; The Wonderful Story of Henry Sugar and Six More; The Twits;* and his screenplay of Ian Fleming's *Chitty Chitty Bang Bang* proved that Dahl knew a great deal about what young people like.

According to Dahl, "the writer for children must have a really first-class plot. He must know what enthralls children and what bores them. They love being spooked. They love suspense. They love action. They love ghosts . . . . They love seeing the villain meet a grisly death. They love a hero and they love the hero to be a winner."

From the start a good writer, and thanks to his children, a good writer for young people, Dahl still finds some things hard. "To me the most important and difficult thing about writing fiction is to find the plot. Good original plots are very hard to come by. You never know when a lovely idea is going to flit suddenly into your mind, but by golly, when it does come along, you grab it with both hands and hang on to it tight. The trick is to write it down at once, otherwise you'll forget it. A good plot is like a dream. If you don't write down your dream on paper the moment you wake up, the chances are you'll forget it, and it'll be gone forever."

"So when an idea for a story comes popping into my mind, I rush for a pencil, a crayon, a lipstick, anything that will write, and scribble a few words that will later remind me of the idea. Often, one word is enough. I was once driving alone on a country road and an idea came for a story about someone getting stuck in an elevator between two floors in an empty house. I had nothing to write with in the car. So I stopped and got out. The back of the car was covered with dust. With one finger I wrote in the dust the single world ELEVATOR. That was enough. As soon as I got home, I went straight to my workroom, and wrote the idea down in a old school exercise book that is simply labelled *Short Stories*."

"I have had this book ever since I started trying to write seriously. There are ninety-eight pages in the book. I've counted them. And just about every one of those pages is filled up on both sides with these so-called story ideas. Many are no good. But just about every story and every children's book I have ever written has started out as a three- or four-line note in this little, much-worn, red-covered volume."

"Sometimes the little scribbles stay unused in the notebook for five or even ten years. But the promising ones are always used in the end. And if they show nothing else, they do, I think, demonstrate from what slender threads a children's book or a short story must ultimately be woven."

With a little red notebook and a vast imagination Dahl has all he needs to weave his splendid stories. He cannot type and so writes with a pencil. In order to imagine his characters, and their outrageous lives, Dahl chooses to write in a place of nearly total solitude and simplicity—a small brick hut in the apple orchard near his home. In cold weather, the hut is heated by a small paraffin stove and an electric heater that hangs from the ceiling above his hands. In an old, cocoon-like sleeping bag, Dahl sits in his hut writing, oblivious to the leaf-strewn floor, the mess made by his nanny goat, Alma, the webs left by his beloved spiders, or the pony and the magpie that come to visit now and then.

"When I am up here I see only the paper I am writing on, and my mind is far away with Willy Wonka or James or Mr. Fox or Danny or whatever else I'm trying to cook up. The room itself is of no consequence. It is out of focus, a place for dreaming and floating, and whistling in the wind, as soft and silent and murky as a womb."

Dahl confesses that he would often prefer to be mucking around in his rose garden, or taking long walks or doing any number of things besides writing. Fortunately, in spite of flying planes, breeding greyhounds and creating terrific orange marmalade Dahl still has enough energy, imagination, and enthusiasm left over for writing—and anyone who has read his books is grateful for that.

Other titles by Roald Dahl you might enjoy reading:

- *Boy* and *Going Solo* are a two-volume autobiography of the author, where he reminisces about his years at a boarding school and his wartime experiences in Africa and the Middle East.
- *Kiss, Kiss* and *Royal Jelly* are both volumes of short stories of the kind that made Dahl famous—fantastic, fast-paced and gripping.

Responding

1. Do you think you would like Roald Dahl's books? Why or why not?
2. Do you agree or disagree with the qualities he says young readers like in a story?

being spooked	ghosts
suspense	seeing the villain meet a grisly death
action	seeing the hero win

3. Do you think Dahl is critical of his ideas when he is drafting them?

FOCUS ON THE WRITING PROCESS

Employing a Writer's Methods

Try out the strategies Roald Dahl discusses in the article.

- Find a place to write where you will be comfortable but not distracted.
- Search through your writer's notebook or journal for a writing idea you filed away in the past. Begin writing about the idea, weaving it into a story complete with real characters, a setting and a plot.
- Try to make the characters "stand out from the crowd" and make them seem as real as possible, so you can enjoy "being with them" while you write. Get involved with them just as you would with friends.
- Try to blot out everything except the characters and the story. Tell the critic in your head to wait till later and let the ideas flow.

Extending

1. Read some of Roald Dahl's stories, including the ones mentioned in the article. What do you like best about his work?
2. How does Dahl's writing process compare with your own? Do you become as immersed as he is in the stories you write?

HOAXED!

Elizabeth MacLeod

Have you ever heard an incredible story, been convinced by someone else that it was true and then found out later that it was all one big lie? Then you've been hoaxed! Hoaxes can be extremely complicated and often require a lot of planning by the perpetrator. They may even involve experts (either real or fake) to verify the story and provide further pressure on the poor victim to believe.

There are lots of reasons why people perpetrate hoaxes. They may want power, money, revenge, fame or improved social standing, or they may hate, love or fear the person they are deceiving. There are also many reasons why people fall for hoaxes, including a desire to believe the incredible is possible, to conform to a group or simply to make money.

Here are some of the most incredible hoaxes ever. Would you have been taken in?

The Piltdown Man

To this day no one knows who planned the Piltdown Man hoax, even though it began in 1908! At that time, Charles Dawson, a local lawyer who was interested in archaeology, found some fossils in a gravel pit near Piltdown Common in Sussex, England. He continued digging and soon uncovered skull fragments and a jawbone. When the bones were finally pieced together in 1912, they seemed to belong to "The Missing Link"—the creature that came between man and apes on the evolutionary tree.

"Piltdown Man," as the skull was called, seemed to be about 500 000 years old. It was named *Eoanthropus dawsonii* after its discoverer and science texts were rewritten to incorporate this amazing find into the theory of evolution. Then, in 1953, a geologist tested the bones and

An artist's reconstruction of what the Piltdown Man would have looked like—had he existed!

found that they seemed to be much younger than half a million years. In fact, it was soon revealed that the jaw had come from a modern orangutan and had been stained with tea to make it look old. The rest of the skull was from a Neanderthal skeleton.

There are many theories about who was behind the hoax, but the hoaxer was never unmasked. One possible suspect is Charles Dawson himself. Other people would like to believe that the hoax was masterminded by Sir Arthur Conan Doyle, the author of the Sherlock Holmes stories.

Dear Diary

Memorabilia associated with Adolf Hitler have always held a lot of interest for some collectors, so forgers have long had a booming business in producing documents, paintings—even operas— supposedly created by Hitler. What made the Hitler Diary hoax of 1983 so incredible was the amount of diary material, the huge sum paid for it and how easily people were taken in.

The German magazine *Stern* and the *Times* newspaper group of London paid more than four million dollars for sixty-two volumes of the diary, which consisted of page after page of almost unreadable scrawl. A distinguished historian verified that the diaries were the real thing, but within two weeks other experts proved that even the paper the diaries were written on didn't exist when Hitler was alive! The real story began to emerge. The hoaxer, Konrad Kujau, had produced all the diaries in an incredibly short amount of time and with almost no research. For background he had simply used a book about Hitler's army that was available in any bookstore and a series of history articles from a magazine.

When Kujau was tried in court, he even wrote up a few more volumes while in the witness stand and created a painting which he finished off with Hitler's signature. When the judge asked him how he could justify these illegal activities, Kujau replied, "But I have to make a living!"

The Cardiff Giant Hoax

Imagine how you would feel if you were digging in a farmer's field and suddenly you uncovered the body of a man over three metres tall! That's what happened on October 16, 1869 in the field of William C. Newell, near Cardiff in New York. The ancient petrified giant weighed almost 1400 kilograms and his body was twisted as though he had died in great agony. News of the discovery spread like wildfire and soon crowds gathered to see the Cardiff Giant.

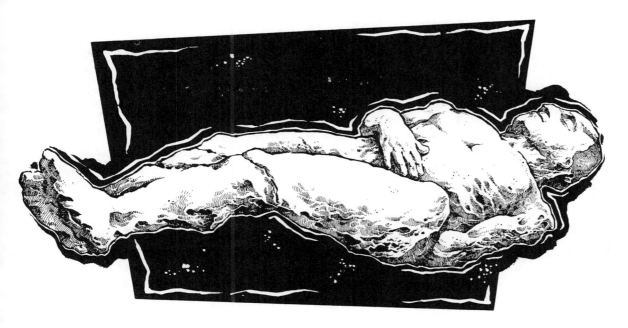

However, a few months later, expert examiners revealed that the giant was actually carved from stone, then dyed with sulphuric acid to make it look old! To give the giant's skin pores the "skeleton" had been hammered all over with needle-pointed mallets. Soon George Hull, a relative of farmer Newell's, confessed to the hoax and said he'd created the giant after hearing a local preacher talk about the Bible passage which describes how giants once walked the earth. But even when it was revealed that the Cardiff Giant was a hoax, people still wanted to see it. Showman P. T. Barnum bought the giant and took it to Broadway where it drew big crowds for some time.

The Hoax that Wasn't

When Scottish explorer James Bruce returned from a four-year voyage to Abyssinia (today's Ethiopia) in 1773, people were amazed by the stories he told. He claimed to have led armed horse guards into battle, been made a governor of a province, nearly been killed many times and seen amazing sights. However, it wasn't long before sceptics decided his tales were *too* amazing, and the explorer became a laughing-stock. Hoping to prove himself, Bruce published five volumes of memoirs. They were bestsellers but only gave people further reason to ridicule and Bruce died in 1794 in disgrace. However, when explorers entered Abyssinia in the early 1800s, they found natives who remembered Bruce fondly and verified all of his fantastic stories. This was one case where truth was definitely stranger than fiction.

A Tall Hoax

Greed is the major reason why people try to hoax others—and it's also the major reason why people fall for a hoax! Patriotism can also be a strong reason. For instance, in 1925, Count Victor Castig called together a group of scrap-metal buyers to let them in on a terrible secret: the French government was forced to admit that the Eiffel Tower was so corroded that it was unsafe and would have to be destroyed. Therefore the government was making available, to the highest bidder of course, the seven thousand tonnes of metal and six million rivets contained in the monument. Secrecy was vital since the tower was a national landmark—*and* because the Count intended to run off with the cheque received from the successful bidder!

When the bids were in, André Poisson was the "lucky" winner. The Count even went so far as to hint that in return for great discretion on the part of Monsieur Poisson he would be awarded one of France's highest honours. Monsieur Poisson was so grateful and so impressed with the responsible way the Count had handled this matter of state secrecy that he insisted on giving him more money. Luckily the Count warned the poor fellow not to start demolishing the Eiffel Tower until he heard from the French government!

The Eiffel Tower, saved from the scrap heap, dominates the Parisian skyline.

April Fool's Hoaxes

April Fool's Day is a great time for mini-hoaxes. Many newspapers and radio and television stations have fun with their audiences by running stories like these.

- British newspapers published a "photo" of spaghetti trees in Italy and showed people harvesting the crop of pasta. Readers tied up the phone lines trying to find out where they could get these amazing trees.
- One Canadian radio station reported that the metric system would soon be used to measure time. The story described how the country would switch to minutes that were one hundred seconds long, hours that were one hundred minutes long and days that had ten hours.
- In 1933, the *Madison Capital Times* newspaper showed a "photo" of the state capitol's dome blowing off, and reported that the destruction was caused by too much hot air generated by state legislators.

Computers now make it even easier to doctor photos, so next April Fool's Day check the newspapers carefully—*don't* believe everything you see!

Responding

1. Why do people create hoaxes?
2. Why do you suppose people suspected Charles Dawson of being behind the Piltdown Man hoax?
3. What do you imagine happened to the reputation of *Stern* and the *Times* after "Hitler's Diaries" were revealed as a forgery?
4. After the Cardiff Giant was exposed as a hoax, people still wanted to see it. Why do you think they did?

FOCUS ON ORAL LANGUAGE

Inventing a Hoax

Work together with a partner or small group to create a hoax.

- Consider something which could conceivably happen, for example, a movie company will be filming on location in your town and needs many teenage extras wearing baby clothes to appear at the school tomorrow morning.
- Appeal to the emotions or needs which make a hoax successful—the desire to believe in the incredible, to be part of something, to conform to a group, to become wealthy.
- Make the details of your tale seem as convincing as possible.
- Spring the hoax at the right time when your "audience" will be at their most gullible and unsuspecting.

Extending

1. Get together with a partner and share your favourite April Fool's trick of all time.
2. Find out more information about the hoaxes covered in the article. Search through issues of magazines and dailies about the time each hoax was revealed.

SCIENCE FICTION, SCIENCE FACT

Jennifer Li

Fantasy fiction isn't always so fantastic. Throughout time authors have used their wildest imaginings to thrill their readers, inventing strange new worlds and contraptions. But in the high-tech world of the twentieth century, many of these writers' weirdest speculations have been made into reality.

Submarines

When French science fiction writer Jules Verne wrote about a mysterious submarine ship named *Nautilus* in his 1870 book *Twenty Thousand Leagues Under the Sea,* no one suspected that eighty-five years later a real submarine would be able to do the same fantastical things as the imaginary *Nautilus.*

The idea of a warship that could attack from under the water had appealed to naval planners for centuries and attempts were actually made in both the American Revolution and the American Civil War to operate submarine boats propelled by muscle power. However, it wasn't until the age of electric motors, like those that powered Verne's *Nautilus*—that the submarine made its real debut. Fact met fiction in the early days of World War I, when in one afternoon a single German submarine sank three large British warships, one after the other.

The power and menace of submarines increased through both world wars, but the real meaning of the word submarine (underwater) wasn't fulfilled until nuclear power made these ships capable of travelling unlimited distances under the oceans at high speeds—without coming up for air or to recharge batteries. In the mid-1950s, the U.S. Navy developed a submarine that could travel the world submerged, even under the polar ice caps—just like Jules Jerne's *Nautilus!* Out of respect for Verne's prediction, the navy submarine was called—you guessed it—the *Nautilus*.

Television

As with so many other twentieth-century innovations, Jules Verne was the first to "invent" television—in his imagination, of course. Although a medium that could transmit voice and pictures through space had been dreamt about for centuries, Verne wrote about an actual device in his 1875 book *In the Twenty-Ninth Century.* Twenty years later, that other great science-fiction prophet, H. G. Wells, also wrote about a form of television in his book *The Time Machine.*

The discovery that made television possible was made by Albert Einstein. He was awarded a Nobel Prize in 1921 for his work on the "photoelectric effect," which is the primary principle behind the television picture tube. After that, it was only a matter of time before a commercial application was found. Television was experimented with in the 1920s and the first sets were available in the late 1930s. Not until the early 1950s, though, did the medium begin its explosive expansion into everyday life. Even Jules Verne and H. G. Wells could not have imagined how many people would one day have television in their own homes.

Atomic Energy

In his Special Theory of Relativity Einstein posited that every particle of matter represents an immense amount of energy. In his 1914 book *The World Set Free,* the English scientist, writer and philosopher H. G. Wells pointed out that civilization could be transformed if the energy found in the nuclei of atoms could be harnessed and controlled to provide a steady flow of power.

In the 1920s and 1930s, scientists worked to control the release of energy from the unstable nuclei found in heavy radioactive elements like uranium. In the atmosphere of the Second World War, the American and British governments were eager to be the first with controlled nuclear power that could be used for weapons and a huge crash program was begun. In 1942, in an underground lab under the main football field at the University of Chicago, scientists finally started and controlled a nuclear chain reaction.

Albert Einstein, the physicist whose work made television possible.

The heat from the chain reaction could be used to generate steam to power turbines, which in turn could generate electricity: Wells's prediction in *The World Set Free* had come to pass.

Lasers

The "death ray" common to villains in early science fiction is one of the more destructive fictional predictions for the laser beam. The use of an intense beam of light to cut and drill things was imagined by the great Elizabethan philosopher and scientist Sir Francis Bacon in the seventeenth century. When the laser was invented in 1960, fantasy became fact: powerful beams of light could now be used for medical purposes.

Lasers produce a highly concentrated beam of energy which travels in a completely straight line. Because of this, they can be used for surveying and measurement. They also focus energy so precisely that they can be used in very delicate surgery, vaporizing tissue in places a knife could never reach. Recently, lasers have caused giant changes in the communications field—laser beams have been used to transmit television programs, and compact discs are played by lasers which read the information on the disc.

Artificial Intelligence

Machines that can think are an idea which science fiction writers have returned to time and again. The writer Aaron Nadel, for example, wrote a story called "The Thought Machine" in 1927. Modern microcomputers can perform amazing calculations at incredible speeds—a pocket calculator has all the power of the first huge computers of the 1950s that filled rooms. Currently researchers in both the United States and Japan are working on a "supercomputer"— a machine that could duplicate the human mind.

It remains an open question whether computers will ever really duplicate human thought. Our minds are so complex and creative, work so fast and can store so much, that no current computer could even come close to matching our capabilities. Nevertheless it is sure that even science fiction writers would have found it difficult to imagine how many people would actually own their personal "thought machines" powering such things as watches, microwave ovens and pocket calculators.

Robots

Robots were first mentioned by the Greek poet Homer, who wrote in the eighth century. In Homer's most famous poem, the *Iliad*, the god of metalworking and fire, Hephaestos, is attended by golden tripods which move by themselves wherever he wants them to go. Greek mythology also refers to a bronze giant named Talos who defended the island of Crete.

In eighteenth-century Europe, machines and dolls run by clockwork were much admired. The German writer E. T. A. Hoffman wrote stories about mechanical people who came to life in disturbing ways. It was only after electrical power became more widely used that science fiction writers began to imagine automatic people made of metal and powered by electricity. In 1921 the Czech writer Karel Capek coined the word "robot" in his story "Rossum's Universal Robots."

Microprocessors are now capable of powering machines that can perform complex operations once believed to be impossible. Advanced robotic technology is more likely to be used to make a factory arm than a human-shaped machine; but research continues and one day it may indeed be possible to create the perfect robot servant that Homer imagined over twelve centuries ago.

Responding

Which invention mentioned in the article

- carries the most potential danger?
- interests you the most?
- has the greatest impact on warfare?
- is the most useful to scientists?
- has had the greatest impact on the everyday lives of people?
- can save the most lives?

FOCUS ON COLLABORATIVE LEARNING

Discussing

Get together with a group of four or five other students to interpret and discuss the following quotations about imagination. What does each quotation mean? Do you agree with the idea expressed?

Artists treat facts as stimuli for imagination, whereas scientists use imagination to coordinate facts.

Arthur Koestler

He who has imagination without learning has wings and no feet.

Joubert

Solitude is as needful to the imagination as society is wholesome for the character.

J. R. Lowell

There are not days in life so memorable as those which vibrated to some stroke of the imagination.

Ralph Waldo Emerson

Imagination grows by exercise and contrary to common belief is more powerful in the mature than in the young.

W. Somerset Maugham

Extending

1. Get together with a partner and brainstorm other inventions which have had far-reaching effects. What is your favourite invention of all time?
2. Read Jules Verne's *Twenty Thousand Leagues under the Sea* or obtain the video and watch it with a group of other students. What did you think of the *Nautilus?* How did it compare with modern submarines?

RECOLLECTIONS

As recently as 300 years ago, 150 vertebrate species of animals that have now become extinct walked the earth.

Teddy bears were named after the U.S. president Theodore "Teddy" Roosevelt, who enjoyed bear hunts in his spare time. Ken and Barbie dolls were named after the children of their inventors, Ruth and Elliott Handler.

A child of six knows about 3000 words. An average adult has an active vocabulary (speaking or writing) of ten to twenty thousand words, and a passive vocabulary (reading or listening) between thirty- and forty thousand.

FABULOUS FADS!

Elizabeth McLeod

Hula Hoops, Rubik's Cubes, Pet Rocks—no, they're not weird new cereals, they're all fads, those wonderfully wacky items or activities that suddenly become incredibly popular; then, just as quickly, disappear into oblivion.

Why do people get so involved in fads? Probably the biggest reason is a desire to try new things and to be seen as always being up-to-date. Other reasons include influence of friends or people you're trying to impress—most of us like to be one of the gang. Whatever it is, it obviously works, since new fads spring up almost daily.

Here are a few of the biggest fads ever.

CB Radio

The CB (Citizens' Band) radio channel was created in the 1940s and by 1975 about 850 000 radio sets had been sold. But in 1976, when the CB radio fad hit, over twenty-five million sets were sold in that year alone. The CB radio craze resulted in movies, songs and a TV series, as well as such inconveniences as leaked signals affecting TV signals and opening garage doors. You probably already know some of the phrases that crept into everyday usage from this fad. Phrases like "10-4" meaning "okay," "cotton pickers" for "non-truck drivers," "double nickels" meaning "55 mph speed limit," and "good buddy" meaning "friend." English experts worried that this fad would cause permanent damage to the English language, but by the end of 1976 the CB craze was over and those weird terms completely dropped from our language, good buddy.

The Hula Hoop

This toy became popular in 1958 when a sharp-eyed fad spotter watched Australian kids exercising in gym class with bamboo hoops. He imported the idea to North America, changed the bamboo into bright-coloured plastic and one of the biggest fads ever was born. During this fad, about thirty million hula hoops were sold and there were soon variations with bells on them, or ones that went up and down as they went round and round. To keep interest high, hula hoop companies organized competitions to determine who could keep the toy swirling the longest and how many hoops they could keep swivelling at the same time (would you believe fifteen!). Babies, movie stars and even chimpanzees gave the hula hoop a whirl before this fad died.

3D Movies

3D movies were launched in 1952, when movie companies were desperately searching for an innovation to help them survive the onslaught of television. Other gimmicks included wide movie screens, improved sound and even something called Smell-O-Vision! To produce a 3D movie, the scenes are shot with a special camera which simulates how your eyes work together. To do that, there are two side-by-side lenses on the camera shooting the film, each of which represents the sight of one eye. When the two reels of film are projected at the same time in the theatre, those strange-looking glasses with the polarized lenses draw the images together to create the 3D illusion. The films were usually heavy on action and included lunging lions, flying pitchforks, hurtling chairs, etc., which made audiences rear back in surprise and fright.

Critics panned most of these movies, but the customers loved them. However, the fad died when audiences complained of headaches when the movie images weren't projected at exactly the same time—and when they got tired of those glasses.

Mood Rings

What is most interesting about this fad is that it is still around—but in a completely different form. In the early seventies, mood rings, necklaces, even T-shirts, claimed to be able to determine your mood and would turn different colours depending on how you felt. The jewellery was made of heat-sensitive crystals that reacted to your body temperature. Since most people heat up when they're angry or tense, the mood rings usually would change colour and correctly reflect how the wearer was feeling. Nowadays you can buy small cards with a heat-sensitive crystal insert, but in these stressed-out days, instead of indicating your mood, they tell you what your stress level is.

Rubik's Cube

In 1980 four-and-a-half million of these involving, frustrating toys were purchased and in 1981 that figure rose to four times as many! Erno Rubik, a professor of architecture in Budapest, Hungary, created the cube for his students, but quickly realized its sales potential. Rubik's Cube was about the size of a tennis ball and each of its six sides was divided into nine squares, each painted one of six different colours. The object of the puzzle was to twist and turn the squares until all sides were one colour each.

 The craze launched everything from T-shirts and competitions to a sport injury known as "Rubik's thumb." One woman filed for divorce when her husband stopped paying attention to her after she gave him a cube for Christmas. A man got so frustrated with his cube that he ran over it with his truck! No wonder he did: there are 43 quintillion—that's forty-three followed by thirty zeros—possible combinations of the squares on the cube.

Squeezing as many people as possible into a phone booth was a popular college sport in the 1950s.

More Fabulous Fads

How many of these fads have you heard of?

Goldfish Swallowing: This sport was incredibly popular during the fifties, especially at colleges and universities.

Negative Heel Shoes: Unlike conventional shoes, these ones were lower at the heel. The Roots Company made them popular in Canada.

Frisbees: Some people say that this fad was born when someone whipped a pie plate through the air. Frisbees were made by the same company which was responsible for the hula hoop and the super ball.

Pet Rocks: The ultimate low-maintenance pet.

The Twist: This dance inspired songs, TV shows and movies.

Platform Shoes: These thick-soled shoes could be incredibly heavy, but they enabled wearers to "look down" on just about anyone.

Stuffing People in Phone Booths: Another great college sport. At least it was kinder to goldfish.

Responding

1. Does your family have any of the following around the house: a hula hoop, 3D glasses, a CB radio, a mood ring, a Rubik's Cube? What use, if any, is made of them?
2. Can you think of a favourite activity or article of yours which is a current or recent fad?
3. Do you think that any of the fads mentioned in the article would have been as widespread without extensive marketing? Why or why not?
4. Why do you suppose people follow fads? What have you observed about people who follow fads? About those who don't?

FOCUS ON COLLABORATIVE LEARNING

Creating a Fad

Get together with a partner and create a fad. Brainstorm ideas such as the following to get started:

- a new board game
- a lopsided soccer ball
- stilts on springy legs

Give the fad a name and write a description of it accompanied by coloured drawings.

Create a poster advertising the fad and give a short talk about it to the class or a small group.

Extending

1. Do a survey of your parents, grandparents and family friends to find out what fads they remember from the past.
2. Some fads create opposition, perhaps because they are silly or dangerous. Organize a campaign to quash a fad.

   - Name the fad you are opposed to.
   - On what grounds (moral, environmental, etc.) are you opposed to it?
   - How will you go about persuading other people to join you in opposing the fad?

MEMORIES ARE MADE OF THIS:
THE FIFTIES TEEN FASHIONS

Melinda McCracken

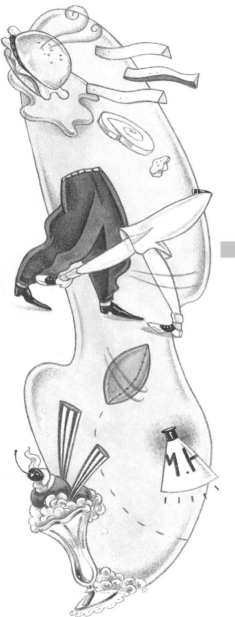

Zoot suits. . .jiving. . .pixie cuts. . .Shocking Pink lipstick. . .In this excerpt from her book Memories Are Made of This, *the author recalls teen fashions of the fifties. Her stories are about Winnipeg, where she grew up, but they could have been about any other part of Canada of that decade.*

The teenager, complete with slang and casualness, could be nothing but an American concept. To be a real teenager, you had to drink Cokes, eat hamburgers (known as nips in Winnipeg, because the local Salisbury House chain, started by R. M. Erwin, an American, in the thirties, sold them as such), French fries (known in Winnipeg as chips, in the English tradition), go to the Dairy Queen, listen to the Top Forty and neck. The realities of Winnipeg, the weather and the geographic isolation, plus the relative scarcity of money, limited the degree to which American culture could be assimilated. Most boys could not afford cars, so did their cruising on racing bikes, and the Canadian teenager's style lacked the voluptuousness of that of the American. But where there were no styles available to copy, teenage ingenuity invented them.

The boys and girls in grades ten and eleven at Churchill were between the ages of fifteen and eighteen, and both sexes had begun the ritual of primping in the washroom. Physical attractiveness was assuming importance all round.

There were two areas of achievement for boys, school work and sports. Whereas the parental attitudes of the society and the school system emphasized marks, sports were far more important to kids because it was in that arena that a boy proved to his friends that he was a man. A boy who wasn't particularly good in school could compensate

Fifties teens enjoy their pop at a soda fountain.

by excelling on the football field, hockey rink, basketball court or baseball diamond. Although sports provided an alternative system of goals and values and fostered teamwork and brotherhood, they weren't any more democratic than schoolwork, because outstanding athletic abilities were as rare as outstanding brains. But they were the field where boys could display their grace and litheness, and decorate the basic skills with their own flair and style, especially in front of girls. So basically there were two types of boys—the brains and the athletes.

The usual dress for ordinary guys and for brains was a plain or plaid shirt over a T-shirt, and sometimes a V-neck or Perry Como sweater, grey or charcoal grey with red and white stripes down to the three buttons at the bottom, cords or chinos and ordinary shoes.

The athletes, however, had a style all their own. They were The Men, the rocks or hardrocks. To them, girls were just a passing attraction. Sports were everything. Churchill High School opened without a football team. Football was expensive, and the support of the business community had to be recruited, and wasn't top priority for a new academic high school. The many good football players in the South End who attended Churchill were pretty miffed. Since they still wanted to play football, they had to go to the west end, out Arlington, and play for teams like the West End Memorials or the West End Rams. Being interested enough in football to go way out there while still going to school meant that guys were fairly independent of the school and of their parents; the guys rejected the implication that football wasn't important, and went on playing. Playing on a team outside the school improved a guy's status, and carried a lot of weight with the girls. From these outside teams, guys got "ball jackets" in the team colours—a Lions jacket was a black Melton cloth windbreaker that fastened with snaps, with white leather sleeves, ribbed wrists and waist and lots of pile in the Lions emblem on the chest and in the lettering across the front. These jackets were a mark of status, indicating that the wearer was "one of the boys." Churchill later issued red, white and blue basketball jackets, but these didn't pack the punch of the originals.

Saturday-night moviegoers line up in front of a Toronto theatre.

The Men were an elite that existed independent of the school. They scorned the school. They sat at the back of the room and goofed off. Schoolwork was sissy stuff.

The Men wore their jackets indoors and out, in class, to parties, bowling, to the show, everywhere, day in and day out. They also wore drapes, a fashion peculiar to Winnipeg, invented and made by the local garment industry for its benefit. The style began about 1950 and ended about 1957. Drapes were like zoot suit pants, wide at the knee and tight at the ankle. The more extreme the ratio of knee width to ankle width, the better the drapes. When the knee was really wide and the ankle really tight, the pants were called balloon drapes. You usually ordered them tailor-made at Eaton's, although there was also a ready-made black denim type with white snaps that was popular. They were expensive, too, and came in a wide variety of checks and colours. You could have one, two or three seams down the side. They were high-waisted, and the belt slipped through wide loops on which you could have one, two or three buttons. The pockets at the back also had flaps that buttoned down with one, two or three buttons; usually if you had three seams, you'd have three buttons everywhere. Some of the back flaps were shaped like gun holsters; these were called gunflap pockets. The girls all had drapes too. They were flattering, in a funny way. In the summer, the boys would wear light unbelted denim pants that were elasticized at the back; this style initiated a fad of pulling people's pants down.

With their drapes, the boys would wear evil pointy black shoes. In winter, they wore rubber galoshes that closed with buckles. It was *de rigueur* to do up only the first two or three buckles nearest the toe, and leave the rest flapping open, so the guys would clink like cowboys in spurs or knights in armour as they walked along.

Boys were very conscious of their hair and combed it a lot. The athletes among the boys usually wore brushcuts because they didn't get in the way. The boys who had longer hair used Brylcreem, which was advertised on sports telecasts. Some of the more progressive boys wore what was called a Bogie or a Boogie cut; this consisted of a brushcut on top, with the sides long and meeting in the back in a ducktail. Bogie cuts had a way of falling forward around the guy's ears, and required a lot of attention to keep that from happening.

The girls still had to wear tunics and white blouses to school three days a week. There was a regulation length for tunics, usually fifteen or twenty centimetres above the knee, which looked awful. Every so often, the phys. ed. teacher would crack down and come around with a yardstick, and make girls kneel down so she could measure how high the tunic was above the knee.

Skirts were based on the torch-singer line; they zipped up the back, were tight to mid-calf and on each side had kick-pleats that flared out like fishtails as you walked. With the skirt, you might wear a Kitten or Grand'mere twin sweater set. You wore them both, with only the three buttons of the cardigan done up, simulating a Perry Como sweater.

Over that, you'd wear a baggy jean jacket that closed with white snaps, much baggier than a Levi windbreaker. Your hair was usually done in a ducktail. You'd arrange curls in front, and kiss curls stiffened with soap at the sides. There were also pixie cuts and poodle cuts and bustles that required permanents. And on your head, in the winter, you'd wear a babushka, a Ukrainian peasant fashion, a silk kerchief tied under the chin. Except you'd wear it pulled way back from your forehead to show your kiss curls, which were often held in place by

Fifties teens listen to their favourite records.

hair clips, as if you were getting ready for something big. "Canoe" shoes, oily brown leather moccasins, were very in; you also might wear boys' black-and-white runners with ankle socks, saddle shoes, and later white bucks. All shoes were worn with nylons with seams in them and white ankle socks, usually rolled down.

Everybody used three-ring binders with leatherette covers that zipped on three sides. Inside you put your Campus looseleaf notebooks, one for each subject, divided by stick-on plastic tabs on which you printed the name of the subject. You filled in the timetable on the front, and wrote your name in the space provided. You put your pens and pencils in the middle of the rings. The school gave out paper book covers with which you covered your textbooks. You put two books side by side inside the binder, and any other junk that would fit, and zipped the whole works up. The rest of the books you'd put side by side on top; you had to take them home with you after four to do your homework, and bring them back to school with you the next day. Soon the looseleaf notebooks would be covered with blotchy doodles from primitive Paper Mates, the covers on your books would get fuzzy and tear and the zipper on your binder would rip from your trying to put too much stuff inside. Some binders developed fantastic character in one term. The guys would clink along with their binder held on their hip with one hand. But the girls carried theirs in front.

Boys would often carry your books for you, or throw them in the snow. Now it was different walking to and from school. Instead of splashing through puddles and walking along the tops of snow ridges, and making snow angels, kids turning into people walked slowly, and when it came time to part on a street corner, they dragged the parting out, standing there talking, stubbing toes in the snow.

From behind our books and under our babushkas, we regarded school with mild amusement, an unfortunate intrusion into our social lives. School wasn't what life was about, but it made all these demands on our time. Still, it had to be gone to, and with a sigh, we went.

Responding

1. How did parents and teens differ in their view of what school was all about? Which point of view do you agree with? Why?
2. Which of the styles depicted in the article would "fit right in" with the styles of today? Which one(s) would look strange?
3. What do you think of the theme of the article—that most teens in the fifties dressed according to the ideal "look" of their day? Do you think today's teens are more or less conformist than those of the fifties?

A Time Capsule

Working with a group of three or four other students, prepare a time capsule to show people in the future how today's teens dress. Consider the following questions and suggestions.

- What striking styles of clothing do you notice among girls? Boys?
- How many different hairstyles can you identify?
- In what way do styles change from summer to winter?
- Are there any dress "rules," official or unofficial, for students to obey?
- Do different kinds of students follow their own unique styles: for example, athletes, serious students, members of school clubs?
- What do students wear for a formal occasion? For casual times?
- What's the current style for notebooks, knapsacks and other accessories?

Make a collection of artefacts, pictures and drawings to show people of the future how your generation looked. Place your collection in a time capsule and display it in the classroom.

Extending

1. Interview parents and other adults to find out how they feel about teenage styles of today. Which styles do they like? Dislike? What are the similarities and differences between the styles of your generation and theirs?
2. Watch a variety of television programs depicting teens. What is striking about their clothes?
3. Choose a period of history which interests you and research the clothing styles of the period. Books, encyclopedias, magazine articles and period movies are good sources of information. What do the clothing styles tell you about the people and their times?

STARTING ANEW IN CANADA

Edited by Barry Broadfoot

These short accounts of the new immigrants' arrival in Canada come from The Immigrant Years: From Europe to Canada 1945-1967. *From war-ravaged Europe, people flocked to Canada in search of a better life in a peaceful and prosperous country. Most of them found it, but for many the beginnings were full of struggle to come to grips with the new experiences.*

Loneliness, the Worst Thing

The worst thing in the first days was the loneliness. You had nobody to talk to. You talked a bit in the shop, but when the whistle blew everybody went back to their homes and you were left alone.

I had a little room in a house on Carlaw Avenue, and I'd sit on this little bed and listen to the radio I had, and when a song reminded me of some other time, I would cry. I cried a lot.

I guess I didn't cry quietly because one day the landlady knocked on the door and asked what was wrong, and I told her I was lonely. She said that was too bad, but why didn't I catch the streetcar and go down where there were the Ukrainian social clubs, the places where men were and played cards? She said she had seen an advertisement in the paper. I didn't know that, because I didn't know how to read English yet.

Next day when I came home from the shops she handed me a piece of paper and said this was the address of the Ukrainian social club where I could talk to people from my own country. She had phoned the *Free Press* and they had told her the address.

That night I went down there, and I knew when I walked in the door it would be okay. There were men and women playing cards and I could understand every word they said. A man came over and talked to me and then he introduced me to some other people, and from then on it was okay. I was living in Winnipeg in Canada where I wanted to be, but I was with my own people, and that was the most important thing.

Clothes, but No Hospitality

The first few months, my husband could only get jobs around Delhi [Ontario] working for other people. We'd got there too late for the tobacco and there was no other farm work, and the farmer told us if we promised to stay until October the first of next year, then we could live in the migrant shack, and we said we would.

My husband said, "Well, we've got to live," and he'd go around to the farmers and they'd give him work, not much, but if he worked three days a week he'd get maybe fifteen dollars.

I had five mouths to feed and I thought, this shouldn't be a problem. And on the weekends we got this farmer's wheelbarrow and a bunch of sacks and we went around to people who had big gardens. We'd ask if we could go over their gardens again. They'd always say yes. We'd find potatoes they hadn't dug, and all sorts of vegetables, and there were lots of apples on the ground that were okay. We'd get a lot. When my husband was working, I'd do it with my little girl. The two other kids, we put them in the school.

Thousands of Europan refugees arrived in Halifax in the decade after World War II.

Women, the ones I'd ask if I could go over their gardens, they'd say, "Oh my, you speak English, so why are you begging?" I'd say, "We are from Hungary." And these women would say, "My, I just can't get over how you speak such good English." I could have said I had been to two universities and I was a biologist and my husband was a music teacher, but we had been in the war for six years. I didn't say that to these women. They were being nice, the way they thought they should be.

"Have you got clothes?" this woman would ask, and I would say, "Yes, some very good ones, but they are in Budapest and I won't be getting them for a long time, because I think the Russians are in my house." Oh, something like that. It didn't matter what I said. These women didn't listen anyway.

They'd say, "What do you need? Where do you live? My husband will drop off some warm clothes for you," and maybe she'd give me some food. Fruit she'd canned or bottled, peas, beans, all these things that Canadian women on the farm seem to do.

Then it did happen, and I was very surprised. Her husband would drive to the farm with clothing and things, and sometimes another car would come, because these women would phone their neighbour and say, "Oh, Myrtle, there is a poor Hungarian family at the McCormick farm and they need help. Anything you can send?"

It was funny. We could have got along easily with nothing from them. I could feed the family very well on the fifteen dollars my husband made. It was hard on his fingers because of the violin he played, but it had been so long I guess it didn't matter. We didn't need their clothes and bedding and blankets, although it was kind, but it would have been kinder if they could have invited us into their homes.

It was too bad, but nobody did. We were just immigrants.

Nothing Could Stop Us

There were plenty of things to do, and you can understand that. We had to get a certificate that we were law-abiding. We had medical checks and interviews with immigration people who were very good, very nice, and they told us we were the kind of people they wanted. It was all very pleasant talking to them, and I've had people say they made too much of Canada, telling them a person would be rich in ten years, but that didn't happen to us. They just said, work hard, don't make fun of Canada and Canadians, obey the law, these kind of things, and we would be okay.

We signed the papers to bring us in, and about eight months later we were on a ship from Bremerhaven along with a lot of other emigrants, and we took the train to Toronto. I remember the first thing I did on

A Hungarian family disembarks after a long sea journey.

the train was buy a Toronto paper which a young boy was selling. All the advertisements for jobs and the pages of Eaton's with all the clothing, and I thought, well, it wasn't a dream. There really is a paper like this showing things they want to sell.

We got jobs in two or three days. They weren't good jobs, but we didn't expect everyone to bow down to us and say, here, please take this good job. I worked washing dishes for twelve hours a day, and Jan got a job in a clothing factory, and it wasn't much like teaching, but we didn't mind. We loved it. We got a room with a hot plate, and we'd buy a big steak and some tomatoes and ice cream, and we'd eat like kings and queens.

We had no trouble. The jobs were just to start us out, and we went to night school and got better jobs, and that is about it. It took us five years to get our own house, one of those boxes, but by then we had become Canadians, and from then on it seemed that nothing could stop us from getting ahead. We were very happy.

On That November Day I Will Be There

I love this country. I just love it. This has always been my home as far as I am concerned. My kids are born here. I am a Canadian, not just a fellow who came from Holland and became a Canadian.

I remember how it was during the war. I was there in Amsterdam that morning in 1945 when the Canadian regiments marched into The Dam and there was the big ceremony and at last we were free.

I am not a member of the Canadian Legion as a veteran. I was too young to fight for the Dutch army, and when I would say to my father after the war that I wished I could have fought, he said to me, "You are lucky you were too young. You would not be talking like that now."

So, on Remembrance Day, every November eleventh, no matter where I am, what I am doing, I go down to the Cenotaph for the memorial service. I do it for the hundreds and hundreds of Canadian boys who died freeing Holland and for the way they were so good to us, helping us whenever they could. I stand there with the people and I think of those days, and I say thank God for the Canadians, thank God for this country, thank God for deciding that I would come to Canada.

I have done well in this country. I have never been on unemployment insurance and I have never been without a job, never in my life, and, on that November day—and I don't care how many Canadians don't show up—I will be there.

Responding

1. How would you feel if you moved to a strange new place where no one else spoke your language? What would you do to cope with the situation?
2. How do you feel when you talk to people who are from a different ethnic community?
3. The people who sent clothes to the immigrant family seemed to be blinded by a stereotype of immigrants. How would you describe the stereotype they held? What was the immigrant family really longing for?
4. Who do you think is typically more patriotic: the teenager who was born in Canada or the one who becomes a naturalized citizen? Why do you think so?

Roleplaying

Assemble a group of four or five students and pretend you are responsible for deciding who qualifies to enter Canada and apply for citizenship.

- Make a list of criteria you will use to guide your decisions.
- Allocate a total of a hundred points among your criteria to weigh the importance of each.
- Assume that each of the four people who told their stories in "Starting Anew" has applied to enter Canada. Roleplay a conference with each applicant to learn more about his or her background and reasons for wanting to enter Canada.
- Judge each applicant according to your criteria and decide on the number of points each would merit. Talk about what you will say to each applicant. What reason(s) will you give each for granting or denying the application?
- Take turns roleplaying a conference with each applicant, informing them about the result of the process.

Extending

1. Find out as much information as you can about Canada's immigration policies. What conditions do people from other countries have to meet to come to Canada as landed immigrants? As refugees? How do people qualify as citizens?
2. You may enjoy reading other stories from *The Immigrant Years* and other books by Barry Broadfoot:

   Ten Lost Years
   Six War Years
   The Pioneer Years
   Years of Sorrow, Years of Shame

3. Interview people who came to Canada from another country to find out what their memories are. How were they treated by their neighbours? What was it like to become established? How have their feelings changed about being Canadian?

THE TRIALS OF TREEPLANTING

By Jessica Pegis

Amy Siamon is a 24-year-old physical education graduate from the University of Western Ontario who spent most of her summers while at university planting trees in British Columbia. "Reforestation" is done in the spring so that the land can return to its natural state after it has been logged. The work is exhausting but rewarding, and Amy says the key to survival on the job is a certain level of physical fitness, a love of nature and the right frame of mind. We interviewed Amy to find out more about her favourite summer job.

Interviewer: *How did you become interested in tree planting?*

Amy: I guess I've always been interested in the environment even though I was doing my degree in physical education. Then in my second year at The University of Western Ontario a company called Roots Reforestation—no relation to the shoe company!—had a booth at the university job fair. They were planting trees out west and wanted students for the summer. I'd been to Vancouver and loved it, so I thought I'd apply.

Interviewer: *Were there any requirements regarding your size or level of fitness?*

Amy: No, there were no actual requirements, although the work is physically demanding. You look at some people and think they would be great, and they don't do well at all. So much of it is a head game—coping with the elements and knowing how much you can reasonably expect to do on a particular day and doing it. There's no perfect physique for tree planting.

Interviewer: *Tell us about getting there and your first days on the job.*

Amy: A couple of my friends had also applied and been accepted, so we flew out to Vancouver just before the planting season—which runs from the beginning of May to the end of June. We were so naive and had no idea what we'd got ourselves into. Then our luggage got sent up to Prince George but we didn't—I remember waiting around in Hazelton all day. When we finally got to the area around Elizabeth Lake, where we would be working, it was pouring, so we got out our bright yellow rain gear and walked into the dining room. Everyone cracked up—it was obvious from our cleanliness that we were new to the treeplanting game, and fashion time it was not!

The next day, we got up around half past five or six—just enough time to organize our gear and get to the block by seven. The "block" is the planting area, and you plant trees in rows according to boundaries that are marked by tape.

Interviewer: *Just so we can picture this, how big are the trees you are working with and where are they kept until you plant them?*

Amy: Until they are used, the trees are kept in cold storage and they're very small. The smallest are pine—they're about eleven cm in height. Spruce trees are bigger, up to forty-five cm; we plant mostly cedar, spruce and pine. The trees are kept cold so that they won't "blush" before they're planted—"blushing" means getting their first growth. The trees are brought to the site on a "trike"—a three-wheeled all-terrain vehicle—and the foreman delivers them

Amy Siamon spent her student summers planting trees in British Columbia.

to the planters. You take as many trees as you can comfortably carry and put them in your belt, which is like a regular waist belt with three plastic pouches called "bags." Then you go to your part of the block—the individual planter's portion is called a "piece"—and start working.

Interviewer: *Do you have to plant the trees a certain distance from each other?*

Amy: Yes, and the amount of spacing that's recommended seems to vary with where you are planting. In British Columbia, spacing is about 2.7 m to 2.9 m per tree. Within a three-metre radius you'd expect to plant about seven to nine trees. In Ontario, the spacing is much closer—about 30 cm. Spruce trees are spaced wider than pines and you plant spruces in wetter area, pines where it's dry.

Interviewer: *Did you become exhausted very quickly during your first weeks on the job?*

Amy: It takes a while before you have enough judgment to pace yourself properly. For example, an experienced planter never takes more trees to the block that she will use fairly quickly—

The planters carry the young trees in plastic pouches attached to a waist belt.

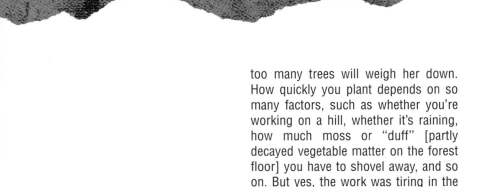

too many trees will weigh her down. How quickly you plant depends on so many factors, such as whether you're working on a hill, whether it's raining, how much moss or "duff" [partly decayed vegetable matter on the forest floor] you have to shovel away, and so on. But yes, the work was tiring in the beginning. It's never a glamorous job and the days are about twelve hours long.

Interviewer: *You mentioned rain. What about coping with the weather when you work outside every day?*

Amy: Actually, the area serviced by the company I worked for was huge, so the weather could vary. Roots Reforestation plants as far west as Harder, Alaska, as far north as Fort Nelson, and right down to the Fraser Valley. Around Fort Nelson, it could get up to forty degrees Celsius. You have to be very careful about sunstroke and wear sunscreen and a hat if it's going to be hot. You take your own water out with you every day and we could drink up to four litres a day and never need to go to the bathroom!

When it's that hot, you also need to keep your trees cool after they've come off the truck. We kept them under "space tarps" that are white on the outside and metallic on the inside. We kept our food and water under the tarp too.

Interviewer: *How much time would you get off from work, and what did you usually do on your days off?*

Amy: We had one day off a week and we would always go somewhere—Terrace, Stuart, Prince George. Our favourite thing would be to check into a

motel and have a shower in a decent bathroom. Then you'd take a long look at yourself in the mirror and see how your body had changed. You become very strong very quickly and develop muscles in your arms, back and legs. It was also nice just to wander around and spend some money. Tree planting is a raw life, so you need that time to relax.

Interviewer: *How do you feel when the season is over?*

Amy: It feels great! We expect that over ninety per cent of the trees that we plant will survive, since we never used any bad seed lots or mouldy trees. Once I happened to go back to the area I had planted in May at the end of the season and my trees had just blushed. It was wonderful.

Interviewer: *Do you have any strong feelings about some of the ecological issues involved in logging and reforestation?*

Amy: It is distressing to visit some of the areas in B.C. that have been logged so extensively that all you can see is cut blocks. Of course, logging companies in the province have to reforest the areas they use now, but sometimes the areas are left too long. Unfortunately, the secondary forest—the poplars and other deciduous trees—can take over and crowd out the conifers. Sometimes the regrowth looks like a jungle—even after you've planted, the duff will come up more quickly than the newly planted trees. Then you have to go back and replant in some blocks. The second-time-round planting is known as "fill planting."

Interviewer: *Would you recommend this job?*

Amy: It's a great job for a university student, since the spring term ends in April and then you still have July and August to take a second job. But it's hard work. Even so, if I had my degree in forestry instead of physical education, I'd go back and look for a job in the industry—nature will always be important to me.

A view of the wooded lakeside at Cranberry Junction, B.C.

Responding

1. What led Amy Siamon to work as a tree planter?
2. What new information about tree planting did you gain from the article?
3. What qualities would a person need to make a successful tree planter?

FOCUS ON ORGANIZING INFORMATION

Making an Outline

Suppose you were about to write an article about treeplanting and were using the Amy Siamon interview to build an outline.

- Write a brief definition of tree planting.
- Make a list of the significant facts about tree planting you gleaned from the interview.
- Study the list of facts to identify the "big ideas" or sub-topics and to see which details or examples support each topic.
- Choose a thesis or main idea for your article. What does most of your information seem to point to? For example, does it say that tree planting is important to the restoration of forests, that it is a good way to make money for university? Each is a different thesis and would take your article in a different direction.
- Make an outline of the information you have gained from the interview.

Extending

1. Imagine that you are writing a book on tree planting and need a glossary of technical terms to help your readers. Create a short glossary using the terms from the interview. With the help of the context or a dictionary, write a definition for each of the following:

gear	piece	space tarp
trike	duff	deciduous tree
block	secondary forest	conifer
blush	fill planting	regrowth

2. Get together with a group of three other students and debate the following issue: "The need to conserve forest reserves versus the need to provide employment for loggers and sustain the economy of logging communities."

   Choose two students to argue each side of the issue for ten minutes. Then switch sides. Which side of the issue received the greatest support in the debate?

The tree-planting crew during Amy's first working summer in 1987.

HEROES & VILLAINS

Unit 5

The "Achilles' heel," meaning someone's vulnerable point, was named after the Greek hero of the Trojan war. When he was a baby, his mother bathed him in the River Styx to make him invincible, holding him by his right heel. Achilles died when an arrow struck his heel, the only part untouched by the magic waters.

The most villainous Hindu deity is the goddess Kali. She is usually represented wearing a necklace of human skulls.

POLAR DARE

Priscilla Turner

The fourth polar bear was Helen Thayer's biggest problem. On her way to the North Magnetic Pole in April 1988, Thayer had already persuaded three of the giant hunters to go off and look for an unwary seal, rather than eat her and her obnoxious flares. But the fourth bear was not the subtle type. He charged from behind an iceberg, went for her eighty-kilogram sled, flipped it and started towards her.

"In that moment I realized that all I had learnt meant nothing," says Thayer, a fifty-one-year-old climbing guide from Snohomish, Washington, "that in the face of that magnificent, killing creature, my gun might as well have been a toothpick and that I was no more important than the tiniest speck of snow. I knew if he got my head in his mouth, there'd be a very loud crunch."

Never mind cold so bitter it shattered canisters of film, winds that knocked Thayer flat and the eerie feeling of navigating on sea ice out of sight of land. The worst thing about Thayer's 550-km, 27-day trek were the bears, who move silently on thick padded paws and rarely come across anything on the ice that isn't a potential meal. Helen had expected to face them all by herself. But before she left her base camp on Cornwallis Island in Canada's Northwest Territories, an Inuit polar bear hunter gave her a guard dog, a big, black Husky/Newfoundland mix, whom she named Charlie.

It was Charlie who staved off the terminal crunch. As the fourth bear lowered for his charge, Thayer released the dog, who grabbed the bear by a hind leg and started him spinning like a furry planet. The huge beast took off as soon as he could. Charlie followed in rabid fury, leaving Helen to consider what it would have been like to make her trek absolutely, completely alone.

Helen Thayer hugs Charlie, her Huskie/Newfoundland companion on the 1988 trip to the Magnetic North Pole.

In spite of the bears, Helen Thayer eventually became the first woman—and one of just two people in recent history—to ski solo to the North Magnetic Pole. The remarkable thing about her achievement is that she made it without the back-up of sled dogs, snowmobiles or major sponsorship. This sets her apart from many recent polar expeditions backed by large networks and lots of money.

Perhaps the most extreme contrast to Thayer is the Japanese film star who headed for the North Pole with guides and a small flotilla of snowmobiles as a publicity stunt. She never made it. Even more seasoned and respected adventurers have taken comforts where they could. When Frenchman Jean-Louis Etienne skied to the true North Pole in 1986, his crew flew in everything from sleds to soap on five separate occasions. A friend dropped by for a visit, bringing smoked salmon.

As Thayer skied steadily north towards her goal, she left prime bear territory behind, but not the cold facts of travelling in the High Arctic. In Arctic temperatures, elastic straps stretched out and never snapped back and frost formed on Thayer's eyelashes. Violent storms confined her to her tent for up to five days at a time. Once her fingers were so cold she used her elbows to set up her stove and nearly burned down her tent.

And there were the smaller idiosyncrasies of Arctic life: Thayer let Charlie eat out of her dish after his got banged up and blew away; she didn't change her clothes for twenty-seven days; she had to slit the hem of her jacket to release ice formed from frozen condensation. And she had to make sure that her diary, logbook and exposed film were stowed in separate parts of her gear—if a bear got her and thrashed through her supplies, there might be at least some hope of recovering a partial record of the expedition.

Thayer threw herself at the high Arctic with very little margin for error. Her "crew" consisted of an Arctic outfitter in Resolute, Cornwallis Island, Canada, who listened for her radio reports every night and her sixty-one-year-old husband, Bill, a pilot who would have gone with her if there'd been enough money. Instead, he went to Florida and dusted crops to help cover the expedition's $10 000 cost. Thayer was so broke at the end of the trip that she couldn't afford to have her sled freighted back home with her.

Helen Thayer does not like to talk about fear even though she's spent a lifetime facing it. She's survived expeditions when others have been lost, but she's as unwilling to talk about these tragedies as she is to linger over her accomplishments. And those are considerable: since her fortieth birthday, she has climbed both the highest mountain in North America, Alaska's 6 200-m Mt. Denali, and the tallest in the Soviet Union, 24 000-m Peak Communism. This says nothing of previous exploits on the high volcanoes of Mexico and South America.

If you press her about the trials of her adventures, she'll change the subject to the family she met when she was climbing in the Pamir Range of Central Asia. She left the rest of her party, hiked 22.5 km down to an idyllic valley and spent the night in a dirt-floored *yurt* with a Tadzhik clan. "We didn't speak each other's language," Thayer says, "but the teenage daughter cried when she saw me getting ready to go."

Like many other accomplished climbers and adventurers, Thayer would rather discuss "working through fear" than the great panicky abyss itself. She considers a terrifying situation a set of problems that must be solved on a very tight deadline. "I just figure out what the steps are," she says with the discipline of a soldier or an athlete, "and get the job done. If it doesn't have to do with the thing before me, I don't let myself think about it." Perhaps it's this unwillingness to ponder the ultimate consequences that saves Thayer's neck. Consider the time, near the end of her expedition, when a sudden catastrophe just about did her in.

Storms in the high Arctic usually are not blizzards. Thayer remembers how strange it was to see the sun burning in a blue sky overhead, when the temperature dropped and airborne ice crystals glazed the horizon. Not much snow falls in these icy, arid reaches, but the winds, with nothing to stop them, shoot along at speeds exceeding 120 km per hour.

"These storms would blow up out of nowhere," explains Thayer. "You barely have time to react." One afternoon, Thayer had just stopped to set up her tent for shelter, when a sudden blast blew by her, taking with it much of her food and fuel. She reached out and grabbed what she could, miraculously snaring Charlie's chow. Then a sideways gust knocked Thayer over, jarring loose her goggles. As she turned to see how Charlie was faring, the wind drove ice crystals into her right eye, virtually blinding her. Thayer managed to reach Charlie and huddle with him behind her sled for about two hours, waiting for the winds to dissipate. "Frankly," says Thayer, "I was a little bit worried we'd freeze to death right there."

Nearly blinded by airborne ice crystals, Helen attempts to set up her tent for shelter.

Eventually the storm subsided and Thayer took inventory. All that remained of her food was a store of walnuts, which she divided into piles, then smaller piles, to gauge how many days of travel the meagre supply would support. "You see, I knew I was almost at my goal. There was no point in radioing in and saying 'Come pick me up.' They couldn't have even if I'd wanted them to. I had to get to the place where I knew they could land," explains Thayer.

In spite of her injured eye and paltry rations, Thayer kept on travelling towards, around and possibly even over the North Magnetic Pole. Unlike the true pole, the North Magnetic Pole does not sit benignly at the top of the world. Some 970 km to the south, it wanders like a refugee, roughly scribing an ellipse that may vary from 65 to 240 km in a single day, depending upon magnetic disturbances deep under the earth's surface. Thayer covered the entire North Magnetic Pole area; she used her watch, sun tables and the sun itself to navigate because magnetic forces in these remote regions render compasses useless.

For several days, she couldn't see well enough to make out her charts, so she relied on the pathfinding method Inuits have been using for years, following the *sastrugi,* long wavelike ridges in the ice formed by prevailing winds. "And when I couldn't see those, I just went by the feel of the wind on my shoulder," she says.

By the time the 161.5-cm former discus thrower and sled racer reached her pickup point on Helena Island, she was dead sure she'd nailed the North Magnetic Pole. Then she warmed the batteries for her radio against her ribs, extended the 30 m aerial and called for a plane to come pick her up. The pilot, who arrived the next day, gave Thayer his sandwich (for a week she'd been telling Charlie that he might just have to start sharing his chow). Thayer kept something else the pilot had given her—a $1 623 bill that certifies Thayer has actually been to the North Magnetic Pole.

Though she hopes to scale Mount Denali once more before the decade is out, Thayer hasn't finished exploring the Arctic yet. The North Magnetic Pole trip was just warm-up. Thayer and her husband, Bill, plan to make an expedition to the true North Pole next year; they are determined to do it without re-supply or backup of any sort. If they're successful, they hope to tackle the South Pole next.

In the meantime, Thayer isn't losing any ground. She does hour-long workouts on a homemade weight set every morning at five, hauls a sled up the steep wooded hills behind the corral where she keeps five amiable goats and squeezes in a daily 16-km run with her faithful friend Charlie, who is still learning the ropes of living in a house. The first time Thayer left him alone at home, he tried to chew his way through the kitchen door. But that was nothing compared with his reaction when he saw the image of a polar bear during one of Thayer's slide shows. "He did his rabid-dog routine," explains Thayer. "He wouldn't let me near the screen."

Responding

1. Imagine that you were Helen Thayer's friend and she told you she was thinking of hiking alone to the North Magnetic Pole. How would you react to her plan?
2. If you were telling someone else what Helen Thayer is like, what would you say?
3. What role did Charlie play in Helen's expedition? Do you think she would have been successful without him? Why or why not?

FOCUS ON READING

Reading a Challenging Article

When you know the article you're about to read is of more than average difficulty, it pays to approach it systematically. Try the following approach which compares reading an article with taking a trip through unfamiliar territory.

- Size up the territory first. Look over the article to get a general impression of what you'll be reading.
- Make a mental map of the article including the destination you want to reach. What guidelines can you rely on: title, subtitles and so forth?
- Keep your eye on your destination. Concentrate on the purpose you're reading for, the main idea you're looking for.
- Take extra time going over the rough spots. Study unfamiliar words to see if their context helps you understand them.
- Try naming the landmarks you come across. If you detect the sections according to which the article is organized, try naming them as you move along.
- When you get there, look back over where you've been. Did the article answer your questions? How do the various parts of it fit together? What did you learn about the topic?

Extending

1. Imagine that Helen Thayer has agreed to speak to your class about her journey to the North Magnetic Pole. You have been chosen to introduce her. Write down what you would say about her.
2. Locate other stories about heroic expeditions such as the first successful ascent of Mount Everest and read them.

CUDJOE AND NANNY, HEROES OF THE MAROONS

Kat Mototsune

In 1875, a group of more than five hundred men, women and children arrived in Halifax, Nova Scotia. They were the Maroons. Deported from Jamaica, they were forced to leave the land where they had fought for freedom from English slavery for a hundred and fifty years. After five long, cold years in Halifax, these refugees won their petition to be transferred to Sierra Leone in West Africa. In West Africa the Maroons were near the land of their ancestors, but far from Jamaica which had long been their home. They settled there among other freed slaves, passing on stories of their Jamaican homeland and of the leaders of their long struggle in that country. Names like Cudjoe and Nanny were invoked with pride and reverence.

● ● ● ● ●

Jamaica was under Spanish rule from 1494, when Christopher Columbus reached the island, to 1655, when the British invaded. As they faced the British, the Spanish freed the black slaves they had brought from Africa. These freed slaves, and those who had previously escaped into the wild mountainous interior of Jamaica, formed a group that become known as the Maroons, probably from the Spanish word *cimarrón* which means "wild and untamed." The Spanish helped organize, train and set the Maroons against the British. Although the Spanish were defeated in Jamaica in 1655, the Maroons remained a "thorn in the side of the English" until the end of the eighteenth century.

The English brought thousands of slaves from Africa to work on their large sugar plantations. The knowledge that free black people lived in the mountains encouraged many of these slaves to escape to join them. Four times in twenty years the slaves rebelled; some escaped and joined the rebels' towns. When a slave ship from Madagascar wrecked on the Jamaican coast, the survivors joined the Maroons. Although a small group of Maroons signed a treaty with the English in 1663, by the end of the seventeenth century there were about two thousand rebel Maroons on the island, warring with the British to retain their independence.

The Maroons were divided into two groups. One group lived in the Blue Mountains in the northeast of Jamaica. They were known as the Windward Maroons, for the prevailing winds that blow on the northeast coast of the island. The other group of Maroons lived in the northwest section of the island: they were known as the Leeward Maroons, or the Trelawny Maroons. Their greatest hero was a military leader named Cudjoe.

Cudjoe was a Coromantee slave from what is now Ghana. The Coromantee people were known for being courageous and warlike and Cudjoe was fierce and shrewd. He united the Maroons from several African bands—from Ghana, Nigeria, Dahomey, Madagascar—and under his leadership they became excellent guerilla warriors. They swooped down from the hills to raid plantations and then disappeared back into the difficult terrain. They became expert shots with muskets. The rough, mountainous country where they had been forced to retreat became their greatest advantage: they learned to move quickly and quietly over the rocky ground and became skilled in travelling through untracked forest. The British

tried to rout Cudjoe's people with Indian trackers, dog handlers from Cuba, the militia and finally two regiments of regular soldiers—all without success.

It wasn't until the 1730s that the British discovered it was difficult for Cudjoe and his people to get food. The Maroons cultivated hidden provision grounds to grow what they needed. The English governor's men were sent in greater and greater numbers to destroy the Maroon provision grounds and to cut off any other supplies of food and water.

Cudjoe led the Leeward Maroons westward into an area of Jamaica known as the Cockpit Country. A large plateau of limestone, where deep ravines and sinks separate saw-toothed ridges of rock and where the trees grow straight out of stone, the Cockpit Country provided Cudjoe and his people with a secure stronghold, which could only be reached through narrow, easily defended passes. Their *abengs*—shell or cow-horn trumpets—allowed the Maroons to send coded warning messages over long distances.

But the Cockpit Country was very dry and the English soon cut off the Maroons' sources of water and food. Cudjoe knew he had to change tactics to save his people. In 1739, the British finally offered to make a treaty with Cudjoe. Cudjoe met with the English officer, they exchanged hats as a sign of friend-

The British sign a peace treaty with the Maroons.

A Maroon captain.

A contemporary engraving of Trelawney Town, the chief residence of the Trelawney Maroons.

ship and agreed to a treaty which gave Cudjoe's people liberty and large swaths of land. Cudjoe and his successors were empowered with complete jurisdiction over their people, except for death penalty. For a time, it looked as though the Trelawny Maroons could live with what Cudjoe had won for them.

•••••

The other group of Jamaican Maroons, the Windwards, established themselves high in the Blue Mountains, and near a waterfall they built their centre—Nanny Town. The male leaders of these Maroons included Cuffee, Quao and Adou, but it was Nanny who, as *obeah*-woman or high priestess, inspired spiritual power and unity. Many of the British records present Nanny as a legend or give brief mention of her as a Maroon religious woman, but her name entered the Jamaican language in several terms—Nanny Town, Nanny thatch,

Nanny pot, Nanny Hill, Nanny River—giving us some idea of her importance to the Windward Maroons. Her story inspired many stories of her supernatural powers. There is a legend of the Nanny pot, or cauldron, which boiled without fire, and was said to attract and drown any English soldier who approached Nanny Town. It was also said that Nanny could catch enemy bullets and fling them back at the attackers to kill them.

The Windward Maroons were more self-sufficient than Cudjoe's people and cultivated the valleys where they lived. Like the Leeward Maroons, they used the high territory to their advantage, inhabiting natural fortresses. Without as much need to raid plantations for supplies, Nanny's Maroons held fast against the British as much through their united spirit and culture as through their battle strategy.

They managed to hold off the British troops until 1734, when the English dragged small swivel guns up the steep mountainsides and blasted Nanny Town to the earth. Nanny was among the few survivors.

As warlike as Cudjoe, Nanny led her people into battle with the English. She was even said to be able to spirit the best slaves out of their bondage. Nanny's people responded to her religious authority: their faith in her kept them united in battle and her bravery has been kept alive by the Maroon people, to whom she is as much a hero as Cudjoe.

Most survivors of Nanny Town continued their fight for independence under the leadership of Quao. Only three months after Cudjoe signed his treaty in 1739, Quao made a similar agreement with the British. Nanny's status as a political leader and her determination to retain independence are indicated by a separate treaty that the British agreed on with Nanny, a full year after those signed by Cudjoe and Quao. Nanny and her people received similar rights as the rest of the Maroons—freedom and land.

●●●●●

The Maroon treaties of 1739-1740 seemed to uphold an uneasy peace for about fifty years. But the Maroon people were neither as independent as they wished, nor as free as they had been. The land granted the Maroons was not expanding to keep up with the growing population and it was better suited for warfare than for agriculture. Maroon villages were supposedly self-ruled, but each was assigned a white superintendent. Worst of all, the British expected the Maroons to help in their hunt for runaway slaves, and this horrible activity was their only source of income. In 1795, the second Maroon War broke out as the Maroons demanded more rights from the English. But this time there were no heroes like Nanny and Cudjoe to lead them. By means of a trick truce and a broken promise that no Maroon would be forced to leave Jamaica, the English deported the last of the Maroons from their homeland to Halifax in 1875—never to see their beloved Jamaica again.

Responding

1. Trace the feelings you were aware of when you read the article. Which parts made you feel

admiring?	concerned?
puzzled?	shocked?
curious?	angry?

Writing a Summary

Summarizing is a very useful skill when you're making notes or writing a concluding paragraph for an article. When you summarize a passage, start by jotting down the ideas which are repeated, the details and the examples.

Then try to capture the main idea and restate it as simply as possible, adding just enough further information to make the ideas clear.

Finally, check your summary against the original to see that it is accurate.

Try summarizing the first paragraph or the story of Cudjoe. Get together with a partner and compare summaries.

Extending

Arrange a small-group discussion on the following set of issues.

Many issues relating to historical injustices towards people of different cultures are still evident in society today. Choose an example of an issue that affects Canadians and research it through the media. In a group discussion, explore possible ways in which the issue could be resolved.

Alex Scott: Organic Farmer

KEEPERS OF THE EARTH

At a casual glance, the farm of Alex Scott could be mistaken for any of the others that fan out across the prairie west of Virden, Manitoba. Closer inspection, however, reveals a small but significant difference: one looks in vain among the tractors, cultivators, discs and ploughs for chemical-spraying and fertilizing equipment. Scott is a fully dedicated organic farmer, using natural fertilizers, soil revitalization and weed control on his 325 hectares to raise crops that can compete with those of his neighbours. After twelve years of organic farming,

Scott, his wife Bette and their five children are a living rebuke to those who claim that chemicals are a necessity for successful modern farming.

Like many of his generation, Scott, now fifty-one, farmed according to the prevailing chemical and cash-intensive wisdom when he took over the family farm in 1957. He knew farming well, but as the years span by, he became disillusioned with the experience. "It was like being on a financial treadmill," he recalls. "It got to be more burdensome as time went on." Following the oil-price hikes in the early 1970s, the Scotts found that "at the end of the year, there wasn't enough to pay our bills."

Around the same time, Scott became increasingly concerned about his reactions to herbicides, perhaps in part because his son Brett had developed allergies to chemically processed food.

Today, Scott confesses that the break did not come easily. After twenty years of standard farming practices, he had difficulty accepting that chemically dependent, single-crop agriculture was, as he now calls it, "a terminal situation."

In the first years of his experiment, Scott experienced a noticeable drop in crop yields from his sandy, clay-loam soils, something he attributes partially to his own ignorance and partially to the land going through what he refers to as a "withdrawal period." Since then, through trial and error and by tapping into a steadily growing organic-farming resource network, Scott has built a smoothly functioning organic farm.

The lynchpin of the operation is a carefully coordinated crop-rotation regime. "We have to practise a rotation to control disease and weeds and to help the soil," says Scott. The net effect is land that is less prone to wind erosion and more likely to yield a crop in years of scarce rain. Today, says Scott, his farm produces ninety per cent of the district average, without chemicals. It is an accomplishment of which he is proud.

Despite his relative success, Scott refuses to become complacent. Each year he does things a little differently, trying to learn new and better practices. And he now champions politically that which he so firmly believes in. Currently, as president of the forty-member Organic Producers Association of Manitoba, he is working to ensure that the products which are packaged as organically grown conform to accepted organic production standards.

Those standards, says Scott, should reflect what has become for him a way of life. "We have to adapt our way of farming to a sound philosophy," he says. To his mind, crop rotation, soil building and a study of "nature's ways" lead not only to land that is "healthier and more alive" but also to a healthier, livelier farmer. "I'm not going to get rich," he says, "but it's an exciting way of life. Organic farming *is* a viable alternative. For me, it's doing what you like to do and being content. What more is there to life?"

—*Rene Mauthe*

Zoe Lucas: Wildlife Biologist

An isolated, treeless, windswept bar of sand in the Atlantic Ocean off Nova Scotia, Sable Island is home to three-hundred and thirty celebrated wild horses, thousands of sea birds and seals, a six-person weather station and little else. Given as much, one would expect a wild, pristine spot, untainted by the residue of twentieth-century life. And it is precisely for that reason that the beachside rambles of thirty-eight-year-old Zoe Lucas are so disturbing.

Lucas, a self-trained biologist from Halifax who has worked on Sable Island four to six months a year since 1974, devotes most of her energy to studying terrain management and dune stabilization and, in conjunction with researchers at the University of Guelph, the grazing and reproductive behaviour of the wild horses. But on the side, she studies Sable Island's junk.

The junk is mostly plastic and washes up on the island's beaches. Some ori-

Zoe Lucas holds a billed murre strangled by a six-pack yoke.

ginates on the mainland and drifts out to sea, but most of it comes from fishing vessels, commercial and military ships and pleasure craft. It includes fishing net and line, plastic strapping, six-pack yokes, plastic containers, disposable lighters, party balloons and scores of other twentieth-century artifacts.

Scientists estimate that 3.5 million kilograms of plastic are tossed into the world's oceans every year and environmentalists claim that the plastic now poses a significant threat to marine animals. Floating debris entangles and kills tens of thousands of sea birds, marine mammals, sea turtles and fish each year.

In 1986, Lucas, a modest, soft-spoken person fond of outdoor work, started at her own expense a systematic collection of debris, the first study of accumulated marine pollution in Canada. Over three years, she found 11 183 separate items. The message was loud and clear.

"Most people don't see the ocean," she says. "They don't see what's out there. If it's out of sight, it's out of mind. But since it floats, it comes back to haunt you."

To spread her message, Lucas has started to bring Sable Island to the mainland. More of her time these days is spent speaking to students about the high price of marine pollution. Often, she carries along a homemade display adorned with specimens found on the beach, including a well-dried sea bird still hanging from the six-pack yoke that killed it.

As the demand for her presentations grows, her only regret is that it affords her less time on Sable Island, less time with "the sky, the ocean, the dunes, the horses."

But the pleasures of the work, she is quick to report, far outweigh the inconveniences. "It's a great feeling to be able to do this," she says. "Environmental work doesn't have to mean self-sacrifice. The fact is, I can't think of anything I'd rather be doing."

—*Tony Leighton*

Daniel Ashini: Native Leader

While camping in southeastern Labrador last spring, Daniel Ashini and four other men decided to return with their families to their village near Happy Valley, Goose Bay, by canoe, instead of by small airplane. "We took one of the elders who was familiar with the area," says Ashini. "We made our way down the river system and over some of the old portage routes for seven days and nights, sleeping in the open." Then, as they rounded the final bend near home, they could hardly believe their eyes. The entire community had camped on the beach to greet them. Most of the old people were dressed in traditional clothing and a feast of caribou, duck and goose was waiting. "People were crying and dancing and beating drums," says Ashini. "It was the first time anybody had returned by canoe in twenty years."

Ashini, a village chief, tells the story to illustrate how easily a spontaneous act of love for the land can lead to an emotional outpouring. Except for the southeastern camp grounds, almost all unceded Indian territory in Labrador and northeastern Quebec is under siege from low-flying bombers and fighter planes belonging to Holland, West Germany and Great Britain.

Nearly seven thousand training flights a year now originate from the base at Happy Valley-Goose Bay, and the number is expected to more than treble by 1996. If the base becomes an official Nato Tactical Fighter Centre, as the Canadian defence department proposes, the number will reach 26 000 to 28 000 by 2001—nearly seventy-seven flights a day.

"They're turning our homeland into a wasteland," says Ashini, a shy, even-tempered man who speaks directly, with integrity and determination. At the age of thirty, he has become a kind of hero to environmentalists, anti-militarists and aboriginal rights supporters for his leadership of ten thousand of the area's Innu.

Ashini's life story reads like that of many native leaders whose territories are being trespassed upon without prior land-rights agreements: he has struggled to learn new ways to perpetuate the old. Ashini was encouraged in school, where he excelled, advancing to high school in Corner Brook, Newfoundland. After several years in band administration, he noticed a leadership vacuum and coped with his shyness enough to take the top job, becoming not only a village chief, but a key leader for fifteen scattered Innu villages as well. His distaste for the limelight makes Ashini a better leader, not a worse one, people say.

The flights are massively destructive, says Ashini. Jets roar over Innu hunting camps at treetop level without warning, sending children screaming into the bush and dumping paddles from their canoes. Aircraft exhaust can leave a film on the water's surface "like paint," and pilots occasionally release toxic fuel in emergencies. Proposed live bombing poses a forest-fire risk. Furthermore, the activities threaten, to varying degrees, the vast George River caribou herds, large populations of ducks and geese and scarce raptor species such as the gyrfalcon, osprey, bald eagle and peregrine falcon. "This is a life-and-death matter," says Ashini. As flights increase, chances for self-reliance on the land will decrease. If the Innu get no help to adjust—and none is forthcoming—they risk deteriorating rapidly as a society.

Ashini has gone to jail five times for demonstrating at the base and has helped to coordinate a public-awareness programme that has sent Innu families across the country and to Europe. He talked to the Pope recently and joined other Innu leaders in filing a lawsuit to stop the flights—a case expected to last several years.

Whenever he can, Ashini also joins other community members in the bush. "All the senses come alive out there," he says. "It's a very healthy, healing experience. It's important that the land not be damaged. People believe that in their hearts."

—*John Goddard*

Sarah Pugh: Student

Last spring, in front of a flagging audience of parents in Chatham, Ontario, a slender, dark-haired girl climbed the stairs of a school auditorium stage and squinted anxiously into the spotlights. Unlike those preceding her in the city's public-speaking contest—teenagers dressed for success in Sunday-best dresses and suits—eleven-year-old Sara Pugh had turned out for the occasion in a pair of jeans and a sweatshirt with "Save the World" printed on it in bold letters. Over the past few hours, she had listened politely as the other contestants held forth on the subjects nearest to their hearts—homework, younger brothers, music, babysitting. Now, Pugh was ready to take the floor with one of hers.

Staring out shyly into the audience, Sarah Pugh began describing the emerald beauty of a tropical rain forest and the disastrous consequences of continued logging there. "Biologists estimate one species will become extinct each hour by the year 2000 if the destruction continues," she explained gravely. "Already, ten thousand species are becoming extinct every year." Capturing the restless audience's attention, Pugh enlarged on her theme and appealed for donations to World Wildlife Fund Canada's Guardian of the Rain Forest programme. Raising public concern for the devastation had been her only reason for entering the contest: she was terrified of public speaking.

Such unwavering devotion marks Pugh as one of Canada's most energetic and effective young conservationists. Over the past three years alone, the quietly determined straight A student has spent most of her spare hours raising nearly $7 000—penny by penny— for environmental groups. What Pugh has accomplished, writes Senator Rheal Belisle, president of the Canadian Wildlife Foundation, "is an outstanding example of young people's concern for the future of our wildlife heritage."

The daughter of a schoolteacher and an agriculturist, Pugh first revealed her environmental calling at age nine. After watching a television program on the horrors of commercial whale hunting, the Chatham native began reading up on endangered species, becoming deeply concerned about the plight of the peregrine falcon. One of the world's swiftest birds, the falcon had been imperilled by the chemical DDT which was introduced into the food chain by farmers spraying their crops. Even at relatively low concentrations, the pesticide had an insidious effect on the bird's eggshells. "The shells get too thin," explains Pugh, "and when the mother's sitting on them, they break under her weight."

To raise money for a falcon-breeding programme, the nine-year-old stationed herself beside the school's snack bar at noon hours, braving ridicule, to solicit spare change. With the help of her teachers, she persuaded school authorities to hold an endangered species week with school assemblies, penny drives and other fund-raising events. By year's end, Pugh and her classmates had banked $1 100 for wildlife—a sum that was soon matched by John Labatt Limited, when it awarded Pugh a prize.

Encouraged, Pugh went back to work devising new and more imaginative plans. At a class garage sale, she sold books she had outgrown to bargain hunters; in school corridors, she hawked handmade bracelets to classmates. In fact, whenever there was a school event, Pugh was there, collecting coins for endangered species—the grizzlies of British Columbia, the burrowing owls of Saskatchewan or the beluga whales of St. Lawrence River.

Since moving to British Columbia last June with her family, Pugh has doggedly continued her crusade. Already, she has begun collecting silver in her new school and she dreams of becoming a full-time wildlife activist. "There's always some destruction being done," she concludes, sitting on the living-room floor, patting the family dog. "No matter what, you can't save the things that are already gone, and that's discouraging. But there are things you can save and can do."

—*Heather Pringle*

Responding

1. What makes Alex Scott's farm unique? Why did he change his farming methods?
2. Do you admire people like Zoe Lucas for what they do with their lives? Why or why not?
3. What was unusual about Daniel Ashini's return trip to his village? What environmental problems do his people face?
4. Whose needs do you think are more important: those of the Innu and the animals within their territory or those of the pilots in training? Why?
5. How do you know that Sarah Pugh really cared about the subject she gave her speech on?

FOCUS ON WRITING

Writing a Profile

Write a profile of someone whose efforts in conservation have been outstanding.

- Highlight the achievement. Tell what it means to other people.
- Write about the person's character and background. What kind of upbringing and training did your subject receive? What is his/her most striking quality?
- Mention any awards he or she has received.
- Bring the subject of your profile to life. Quote him/her and provide interesting detail.
- End the piece dramatically. Study the profiles you have read for possible endings.
- Read your profile aloud to a small group of other students.

Extending

1. Zoe Lucas is quoted as saying that "Environmental work doesn't have to mean self-sacrifice." Do you agree or disagree with her?
2. Set up an Environmental Achievement Program in your school to recognize the students and teachers who make an important contribution to saving the environment. Decide on the criteria which nominees will have to meet and a selection committee. Think of an appropriate title and token for winning candidates.

A SUBLIME GAMBLE WITH DEATH

John Melady

Y ou won't find the village of Little Red River, Alberta, on the map today, but in early 1929, Canadians from coast to coast came to know its location. A Hudson's Bay company employee there by the name of Bert Logan had become ill: his voice had gone, his throat was paralyzed and his condition seemed to be getting worse. When Dr. H. A. Hamman from Fort Vermilion, about eighty kilometres away, arrived, he took one look at the sick man and knew exactly what was wrong. Logan had diphtheria and if he was not treated immediately, he would never survive.

The diagnosis was all too accurate. Logan was dead even before Dr. Hamman found someone who could take a message for help to the outside world. When he did find a volunteer with a fast team of dogs, he scrawled a quick note, handed it to the driver and told the man to get to Peace River as fast as he could. That was the railhead in those days and a telegram could be sent from there. Hamman had no other way of communicating.

The musher pocketed the note, piled a few supplies on his cariole and disappeared into the bush. It would be two long weeks before the doctor's message would reach Peace River, 480 kilometres farther south. In the meantime, Dr. Hamman treated several native people in Little Red River who seemed to be suffering from the same disease that had killed Logan. Hamman knew that an outbreak of the highly infectious disease, if not swiftly checked, could devastate not only the Little Red River community, but every native settlement for miles around. He also knew that his meagre supply of immunizing drugs was inadequate for the community's innoculation and that his antitoxins were so dated that they were probably useless. If his scribbled

Wop May and Vic Horner with their precious cargo—diphtheria vaccine for the inhabitants of Little Red River, Alberta.

message for help wasn't answered in time, Logan would be only the first of hundreds to die.

Meanwhile, Louis Bourassa was pushing his dog team on to Peace River. After two gruelling weeks he trudged wearily up the steps of the telegraph office and handed the operator the desperate message from the north:

> If possible, rush aeroplane STOP Good landing and no snow STOP If snow, will clear landing strip at both Fort Vermilion and Red River...STOP Send intubation apparatus and several hundred units antitoxin toxoid for two hundred people...STOP Real emergency STOP Do all possible STOP

Wop May emerges from the cockpit of his plane.

Within seconds, it was on the wire to Edmonton, where, less than an hour later, the Deputy Minister of Health for Alberta, Dr. M. R. Bow, phoned Wop May at home. It was January 1, 1929.

May listened in silence, his mind racing, as Dr. Bow outlined the grim situation in Little Red River. May knew he was going to be asked to fly the needed drugs into the hinterland. He was ready with his answer before the doctor had finished. The doctor had only to collect the necessary drugs and May would be ready to leave with them the next morning. Then he phoned his partner, Vic Horner, who agreed to go with May in their Avro Avian aircraft, a small biplane equipped with wheels and an open cockpit.

The prospects for the 960-kilometre journey were incredibly bleak. The temperature the next morning was almost forty degrees below zero. The drugs had to be kept warm. The aircraft had to have a smooth runway each time it landed. The chances of flying into strong winds and heavy snow were reasonably certain—and, most of all, the terrible cold would leave the men in the plane so exposed they might perish on the way. But the young pilot who'd outrun the Red Baron faced the odds calmly.

At noon the next day, he and Horner put gas into the Avian, ran up the engine in a final precautionary check, then took the precious antitoxin from Dr. Bow and placed it in the bottom of the rear cockpit. The drugs were packed around a small charcoal heater, and the heater in turn was wrapped in coarse wool plaid blankets. The flyers were not nearly as warm. Despite heavy clothing, several sweaters, mitts and fur-lined helmets, the bitter cold was penetrating. It was so cold that spittle would freeze into a ball before it hit the ground. But the men clambered into the biplane, and, with a final wave to a few people, May taxied away from the Edmonton hangar and was soon out of sight.

"It was a magnificent flying job," an admiring Punch Dickins tells me years later. "Wop was a good pilot and he did what he had to do. He deserves a lot of credit for that flight." "He could have refused to go," adds Stan McMillan, a man who certainly knew the perils of northern flying, "but it wasn't in his nature to do so. There were so many lives at stake. I am sure Punch or any of the others would have done the same thing."

The tiny silver Avian headed north-west, over the rolling flatland near Edmonton, past dozens of tiny lakes and rivers, all of them frozen until break-up in the spring. Over today's towns: Meadowview, Tiger Lily and Lone Pine. Across the Athabaska River and into the desolate trackless wilderness beyond Swan Hills.

By now, the men sitting in the open cockpit were cold—colder than they had ever been. Numb, barely moving, they had frozen into human statues on a flight that went on forever. Below them, the muskeg and matted spruce; ahead of them the unknown; and without warning, all around them a winter storm that bounced the plane and lashed exposed flesh with the sting of a whip. The tiny windscreens were no protection. The blizzard was everywhere.

May descended for some minutes, trying to get under the storm, to see where he was going, to search for landmarks in a world of white. Every so often he saw a lake that looked familiar, and so he flew on—doggedly, stubbornly—in what he believed was the right direction. Then, as suddenly as the storm began, it abated enough that he could pick out the shapes of buildings, another lake, and yes, on the shore, a crowd of people looking skyward and waving. Ahead, to the left, was a frozen pond and the unmistakable markings of a landing strip between two rows of cut spruce bows. The ice between the rows had been shovelled clean. They had reached the village of McLennan.

The young pilot circled overhead and touched down. By the time he'd stopped the engine, the plane was mobbed with villagers who had heard of the rescue mission on the radio. The strangers helped them from the cockpit and someone carried the precious drugs indoors. Two RCMP officers helped tie a tarpaulin over the engine of the Avian, while Horner drained the oil so that it could be taken inside. He did not even have to let it run into a container. The oil ran out on the snow and froze instantly into a black blob, and the blob was then picked up and removed. Inside, both the oil and the two flyers were finally warm again. After a welcome night's rest, the men were ready the next day to continue their mission of mercy. Shortly after dawn, they said goodbye to the McLennan townsfolk who lined the makeshift runway as May took the Avian off. The next stop was Peace River. There were now 480 kilometres to go.

The final leg of the journey into the north was monotonous and bone-chilling. Mile after endless mile passed beneath the plane. The low hills, the muskeg and the scrubby trees were coated in snow. On the left, all the way, was the ice-covered Peace River, looking as if it were frozen in time.

Choppy air currents tossed the little plane around. Down by his feet, Horner could feel the blanket that was wrapped around the drugs, but he had no way of knowing if they were still warm. He was incredibly cold. His face was raw and he huddled in the cockpit, at times not sure where they were, now and then not even caring.

His partner gripped the controls in hands like claws, tried to navigate as best he could and prayed that the unbearably long journey would end. He didn't know that just up ahead was a cleared runway, a strip of ice on the Peace and a community of anxious northerners who feared that help would never arrive. They had not much longer to wait. Finally, sixteen days after Dr. Hamman had sent his message, the people of Fort Vermilion heard a plane overhead. They rushed to the river.

May landed, taxied the plane to where the people were waiting and cut the motor. He and Horner sat, immobile, frozen, so cold they could not climb out. A pair of husky Mounties stepped forward and clambered up on the side of the cockpit. They grabbed Horner's arms and pulled him upward, then rather awkwardly passed him to others who stood beside the plane. One of the policemen scooped up the drugs from the cockpit floor and a bystander took them indoors immediately. Already, a fast dog team was being harnessed to rush the medicine the final eighty kilometres to Little Red River.

When the Mounties were ready to pull May out of the aircraft, they first had to pry his hands from the controls. Inside the RCMP detachment there was warmth, warmth more pleasant than he had ever thought it could be. And food. Horner and May would remain with the Mounties that night. There had been two gruelling days of flying since the plea for help arrived in Peace River, and now, their delivery done, the two men still faced the trip home.

The weather early the next day looked favourable for flying, but by the time a meagre supply of gasoline had been put in the tank and the hot oil poured back in to the crankcase of the Avian, it was almost mid-morning. There had been a delay in locating fuel, and the little May found was left over from the summer. As he poured it into his plane, he wondered about its quality—yet it was all there was.

Not long after they left Fort Vemilion for the south, the flyers encountered snow squalls and even occasional white-outs. Still they pushed on, because they knew for certain that a landing on wheels, anywhere amid the desolation below, would be fatal. The blowing snow stung their faces and slowly worked its way inside the flight goggles they wore. It swirled into the plane and settled on their arms, knees and shoulders. Neither man bothered to brush the snow away. They were too weary, too cold and too miserable. The flight became an endurance feat that seemed interminable. Then, somewhere, perhaps a 150 kilometres out of Peace River, the engine coughed, sputtered a few times and almost stopped.

May and Horner shook themselves alert and listened to the motor. The sputtering was repeated, so markedly that the little plane lurched in the air, like a car starting in high gear. May sat bolt upright, willing

Wop May dons a pair of goggles and a leather helmet and jacket— standard garb of a 1920s aviator.

the machine to run. He knew now, as he had suspected at Fort Vermilion, that the gas was bad, probably with water in it.

Every few minutes the choking of the engine would stop, but before the two men could relax, it would resume again. Somehow, the flyers felt less cold as they listened in suspense to their erratic engine. They nevertheless were awfully thankful when they saw the Peace River buildings below. They were even more thankful when they landed, the next day, at Edmonton.

In Little Red River, the medication was literally life to those who were ill. The threat of epidemic diminished and in the end only one death occurred. The courage of the returning heroes was lauded in the papers from coast to coast.

As for the dauntless aviators, May and Horner were each given a gold watch and the praise of their peers. Not long afterwards, they flew to California—for a holiday; for the sun; and for a new plane with a closed cockpit.

Responding

1. Why was the outbreak of diphtheria such a serious matter for a remote northern community?
2. Describe the flying conditions that Wop May and Vic Horner faced. If you were a pilot, would you have gone on the mission? Why or why not?

FOCUS ON PERSONAL RESPONSE

Discussing Heroism

Get together with a group of four or five other students to talk about the subject of heroism.

1. Imagine that you are members of a selection panel which gives out an award for heroism. What criteria would you apply to the heroes?
2. Create a brief story about a heroic act and design an award ceremony for the hero.

   • Where would you hold the ceremony?
   • Who would officiate?
   • Write out the "Citation for Heroism" to be read at the ceremony.

3. Exchange stories within your group of heroic acts you have been part of, witnessed or heard about.
4. Who is the greatest Canadian hero of the past twenty years?
5. How does a heroic act affect the people who learn about it?

Extending

1. Find out as much as you can about some of the following subjects:

   • the role of the bush pilot in the North
   • organizations which give out awards for heroism
   • military awards such as the Victoria Cross

2. Create a classroom display called "The People We Look Up To." Include in it pictures of heroes and their awards, collected from the news media.

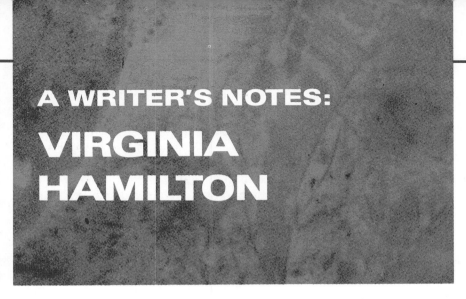

A WRITER'S NOTES:
VIRGINIA HAMILTON

Jessica Pegis

Black American writer Virginia Hamilton says that her
birthplace—Yellow Springs, Ohio—is "the source for all
the fiction I create..."

"My subject matter is derived from the intimate and
shared place of the hometown and the hometown's people
and all that is known and remembered and imagined through time
over time therefrom."

An award-winning author of several novels for young people,
including *Zeely, The House of Dies Drear, The Time-Ago Tales of Jadhu,
The Planet of Junior Brown* and *The Justice Cycle,* Hamilton says that
the longer she remains in her "small village" in Ohio, which was
formerly a station on the Underground Railroad, the more she
understands its impact, and the impact of her family history, on her
work.

"Time and place are so very important to my spiritual self," she says.
"I have suffered through them in the same sense that the black people
have suffered through them toward freedom." Although she enjoyed
fifteen years in New York City, she eventually returned to Yellow
Springs with a conviction that she was reclaiming a heritage that had
been passed on to her "without comment so long ago."

Virginia Hamilton was the fifth child born to Kenneth James
Hamilton, a musician, and Etta Belle, the daughter of a fugitive slave.
Early on, she developed a fondness for exploring "whatever there was
to find," which included the farm country around Yellow Springs, their
neighbours and "my mother's Perry Clan—those cousins, aunts and
uncles whose progenitor had lived in that corner of Ohio since before
the Emancipation."

Living among the descendants of abolitionists and fugitive slaves is
perhaps one reason why Hamilton characterizes herself as "a woman

*Virginia Hamilton, award-
winning author of several books for
young people.*

working, a day labourer." While some writers complain more or less constantly of "angst," a kind of philosophical anxiety that prevents them from filling their daily quota of pages, Hamilton says something occurs to her imagination just about every day. She also says that writing is not easy: "The truth is, the work I do is a long haul day after day from the beginning of a fiction to its end."

She comments that creating fiction often involves discovery. In beginning a new work, she claims to lack the knowledge of the process of discovering the art form that each novel will take: "The work I do is the only occupation I know in which acquired knowledge cannot be applied. What is learned about writing a single fiction is hopelessly inadequate in writing the next, or any others for that matter. Each book is like a new system that must be uncovered. And realizing that I will have to find the system each time I begin is what keeps me startled, awake, through bleary-eyed mornings."

The content of Hamilton's books has been described as everyday events expressed in words that evoke dreams, myths and legends. The author attributes this quality in her writing directly to her heritage, to the black people's "dream of freedom tantalizingly out of reach. . . . Echoes of long past times serve to feed my imagination. They may sound of African dreams or my own family truths." For this reason, her stories have never been known as "play-pretty, to be held, soft and cuddly, in the hands." Instead, her fiction shows how the lives of American blacks have been transformed by the historical experiences which most people only ever read about—"slavery, escape, fear of capture . . . discrimination, and constant despair." However, it is not her intention to "perpetrate a literature of despair, but to present youth an indication of people's range and unique capacity for living."

Daydreams and nightmares have been another influence on her creative life—these, too, form part of the Hamilton family inheritance: "We were all refined daydreamers," she says of her siblings, and "I was a sophisticated 'nightmarer' like my father." One terrible dream experienced for years by Kenneth Hamilton, and later by his daughter, involved "the Faceless One," an entity who appeared out of nowhere and pursued them during sleep. Unlike her father, Virginia says she eventually learned the trick of defeating "the thing": "I flapped my arms and miraculously floated over its head . . . I became a writer, I suspect, at the moment my imagination saw to my rise above the pursuer."

Hamilton describes her current writing regimen as "not strict" and she claims not to think about making books when she is away from the typewriter: "The rest of the time, I'm living and maybe that is the key." She works "no more than five hours at a stretch," saying that the required energy and concentration do not seem to last much longer. Yet she points out that even the frustrating and boring moments of day-to-day existence enrich her work.

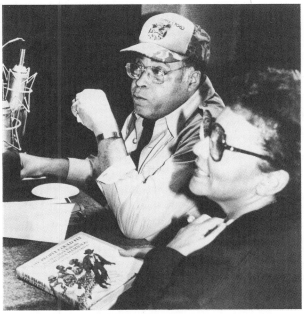

Virginia Hamilton and James Earl Jones narrate The People Could Fly, Hamilton's collection of American black folktales.

In the midst of writing a story, Hamilton is always surprised to find the characters exhibiting their own dynamism. She says she starts "with a fairly clean concept of the story, but somewhere in the midst of it, the story no longer belongs to me. It is taken over by the characters who must live it, who are individuals who change and shape it according to their own will." Still, she acknowledges that there is one note which predominates in her work—melancholy: "I live with a sense of melancholy, which has its origin in black history and life in America. The melancholy sense is an inherent quality of the work, inseparable from the lives of the characters."

Her early characters were well known for their exaggerated physical traits—Zeely Tayber from *Zeely,* nearly two metres tall, the lame Mr. Pluto from *The House of Dies Drear* and the obese Junior Brown from *The Planet of Junior Brown.* These traits "seemed necessary in order to shed light on the characters' inner life and condition," says Hamilton, "but now, my characters have few manifestations of this type." As her writing developed, she noticed her characters seemed to be constructed "inside out from the beginning" so that their emotional reactions, rather than some physical quirk, would reveal their true natures.

Despite her conviction that black literature constitutes "subtle work that cannot be accomplished as simply as other kinds of work with less historical grounding," Hamilton believes that young people should not concentrate too heavily on understanding fiction in a narrow sense. She would prefer to see students read stories with their senses as well as their intellects, so that pleasure rather that understanding is the immediate result: "I suggest that the best way to read is to open the mind and enjoy. Allow fiction to happen to the senses and find happiness. I do."

Responding

1. How do you know that Virginia Hamilton has a strong sense of empathy for her people?
2. How do you feel about her comment that students should "read with their senses as well as their intellects, so that pleasure rather than understanding is the immediate result"? Do you agree or disagree? Why?
3. Hamilton says that writing is a process of discovery for her. What do you think she means by this? Do you have the same experience when you write?

FOCUS ON WRITING

Keeping a Writer's Notebook

Many writers keep a notebook on hand just for the purpose of making a record of the ideas that come to mind. They consider a writer's notebook a place to

- practise new techniques,
- store writing ideas for future use,
- think on paper about things that happen to them,
- have fun with writing.

A writer's notebook is not meant for perfection. You polish the pieces you write for an audience. But here you are free to write for yourself, to dream, to reflect, to ponder your likes and dislikes—privately.

If you haven't got a journal going already, try one for a short period of time—let's say a few weeks. Perhaps writing will become a habit for you.

You might wish to start by writing a reaction to the Virginia Hamilton article, how you feel about some of the things she says about her heritage or about writing.

Extending

Virginia Hamilton knows that the most significant influence on her life and writing is her cultural heritage. Spend some time thinking about your own cultural heritage, perhaps writing about it in your writer's notebook.

- What is unique about the cultural or ethnic group you come from?
- What stories do your family members like to tell about the past?
- What kinds of family or community celebrations are part of your life? What forms of artistic or cultural expression, such as dances?
- Which of these aspects of your heritage could you explore as a writer?

THE MEDIA

A standard newspaper page is no larger than 55 cm by 38 cm because the heavy metal type used to set a page that size weighed about 50 kg—as much as any printing-press worker could handle with efficiency.

The first public demonstration of television was given on 27 January 1926 by the Scotsman John Logie Baird.

The printing press was invented in 1455 by Johann Gutenberg, but he was using principles of wood block printing which had been known as early as AD 704 in Korea.

DO TV PROGRAMS REFLECT OUR SOCIETY?

Susan Smith

Television provides us with a window on the stereotypes that prevail in our society. At this point in the relatively short history of television programming, we may frequently see re-runs of programs that were originally developed in the 80s, the 70s, the 60s and even the 50s. Through these re-runs, we have an opportunity to observe the changes and the similarities in how male/female roles are portrayed, as well as in the presentation of different ethnic groups and cultures and of social and economic groups.

In recent years, the developers of television programs have begun to make positive changes in the range of roles for women, in the inclusion of more of the ethnic groups in our society, and in the characterization of men in new programs, and in basic storylines. But there are many changes and improvements still to be made if we want the very powerful medium of television to reflect the multi-faceted society in which we live.

For example, if you watch night-time TV soap operas, you know how the lifestyles of the wealthy are portrayed. They are white. They live in mansions or luxury condominiums decorated with elegant furnishings and fresh flowers in every room. The characters wear designer clothes and the latest hairstyles. Television "soaps" appeal to everyone's fantasies about having lots of money.

Soap operas not only create stereo-

The stars of "Dallas," the soap opera famous for its images of power and glamour.

types about the rich, they also reinforce stereotypes about people of colour, who rarely see themselves featured in starring or even in supporting roles.

But what about ethnic stereotyping in other kinds of programming? Remember "Star Trek"? This popular science-fiction program was first broadcast in the 1960s and included a Black female as lieutenant of communications and an Asian male as navigator of the starship. It was one of the first programs to include people of colour in integral roles. Thanks to "Star Trek" and other shows that began to break down these stereotypes, we saw a more realistic mix of cultures represented on television. Some of the most popular shows of the

George Takei, the actor who played Sulu in "Star Trek."

Lieutenant Uhura of the Starship Enterprise *crew.*

The cast of "Hill Street Blues."

Gregg Rainwater plays the Native character in "Young Riders," a program set in the American West in 1860.

1980s, like "Hill Street Blues," "L.A. Law" and "Street Legal," offer a more balanced representation of people in the professions from all cultures.

The stereotypical image of Native peoples in the 1800s is also being remade in what we view on television today. "Young Riders," a program set in the American West in 1860, shows new respect for the traditional ways of Native people. The character Buck Cross is played by Gregg Rainwater who is part Kiowa. In one episode, Buck teaches a mute rider Indian sign language and demonstrates skill in identifying animal tracks and tribal arrows which helps in capturing the villains. Perhaps we will have broken down these stereotypes even further when there are more significant roles for Native peoples in

contemporary settings and programming.

Another blatant form of stereotyping is evident in the portrayal of male and female roles in television soaps. One of the most popular soap operas of the 80s was "Dallas." In "Dallas," all the women are beautiful and their make-up, hair and designer clothes are never out of place. They are never overweight, no matter how many gourmet meals they eat. Time and again, women are portrayed as youthful, slim, expensively dressed with a handsome boyfriend or husband. The women who are successful in business are often portrayed as manipulative and ruthless.

The men on "Dallas" are all successful in business, usually enjoying all the trappings of wealth and power. They view women as possessions and decorations rather than people. Interestingly enough, the men are not always young and handsome. There seems to be more tolerance on soap operas for a variety of male characterizations.

It is worth noting that programs like "Dallas" are no longer as popular as they once were. Is it because more and more viewers refuse to watch and support the promotion of racial and gender stereotypes?

Stereotyping of men's and women's roles is not limited to soap operas. It's a fact that, taking all kinds of programming into account, men still dominate our television screens. There are more male characters, and often they have the highest-paying and most interesting careers. If visitors from another planet were to form opinions about life in North American society from what they saw on television, they'd probably conclude that most lawyers, doctors, police officers and career professionals were male.

Women have traditionally played supporting roles as secretaries, nurses and girlfriends. Even though women are graduating from law schools and medical schools in equal numbers to men, male doctors and lawyers still outnumber women three to one on the screen. But this ratio is improving. More professional women are appearing on programs all the time.

The Canadian program "E.N.G.," for example, features a woman as the executive producer of a TV newsroom. She is assertive and independent. She is as intelligent as her male counterparts.

Television news and public affairs programs increasingly reflect the society in which we live. Today, one of the most recognizable people in

Sonja Smits and Anthony Sherwood of CBC's "Street Legal" (above). *Anthony Sherwood* (left).

The principal characters of "E.N.G.," a Canadian program featuring a woman as an executive TV producer. (Courtesy of CTV Television Network Ltd.)

Barbara Frum has been the host of CBC's "The Journal" since 1982.

Canadian journalism is Barbara Frum. Since she first became the host of "The Journal" in 1982, there has been a marked increase in the number of female journalists and anchors appearing on Canadian networks.

Other CBC journalists like Ian Hanomansing and Noelle Richardson provide role models for people of all cultures who aspire to work in network news.

The images of people we watch on television influence the way we look at ourselves and others. We have to watch television critically and recognize its power to manipulate us, as well as to inform and entertain us. Whether we enjoy soap operas, drama series or the evening news, it is up to us to demand programming that reflects an accurate view of the people in our changing society. Intelligent viewing will ensure we get the intelligent television programs we deserve.

Responding

Television has often been accused of promoting stereotypes, a fixed way of seeing things falsely. Which of the following stereotypes do you think television promotes? Name an offending program for each statement you choose.

1. Men have to be handsome and women have to be beautiful to be successful.
2. Women have to be slim and expensively dressed to be attractive.
3. Everyone lives in well-furnished surroundings.
4. North Americans are the most violent people on earth.
5. Men are dominant in North American society.
6. Women are destined to enter lower-paying jobs or get married and raise children.

Analyzing a Television Show

Choose two favourite TV shows, one in the news category and one in the entertainment category, and watch them for several broadcasts.

1. Make notes about the way in which each of the following are commonly portrayed:

   • men
   • women
   • young people
   • children
   • Native people
   • occupations
   • material things

2. What stereotypes did you notice regarding

   • male roles?
   • female roles?
   • ageing?
   • minorities?
   • standards of living?

3. What do you think is the effect on the viewer of repeated exposure to these stereotypes?

Extending

1. Why do you think TV shows make so much use of stereotypes instead of showing us how things really are? Discuss some of the following reasons with a partner.

   • It takes less effort to fall back on stereotypes than to create new stories and real characters.
   • The viewing audience expects familiar ideas and kinds of people on television.
   • The use of stereotypes helps sell products for advertisers.

2. Get together with a group of other students and discuss how you would go about combating the stereotypes mentioned in the article.

THE STORY OF A STORY

Alison Dickie

Denise is the last reporter in the newsroom. She is just finishing what she thinks is her final story of a long day when the call comes in. A train reported to be carrying dangerous chemicals has been derailed just outside the city.

During the 45-minute ride, Ken loads his cameras with new film and checks over all of his equipment. Denise flips on the radio to catch reports from the scene of the accident—a local radio reporter is already at the scene. There doesn't seem to be any agreement on what kind of chemicals are involved and no reports on whether anyone has been injured.

The city editor assigns Denise to the story and asks Ken, one of the paper's photographers, to accompany her to the site of the accident. Within minutes the two are on the highway out of town in one of the paper's staff cars.

When they arrive at the scene, Denise and Ken make their way
to the police officers standing by three waiting ambulances. The
area around the wrecked train is already cordoned off by long
yellow road blocks.

Ken begins taking pictures at once. He has to use a zoom lens
to get close-ups, since he cannot go past the barricades. After
showing her press pass, Denise begins asking the chief officer
questions. Ten minutes later, a local television crew arrives to
film the scene.

Denise asks the police officer why the train derailed. The officer
says she won't know until a railway inspector shows up. She
also tells Denise that no one can talk to members of the train
crew until they have spoken to a railway official and to the railway's lawyers.

A short time later the officer calls Denise over to tell her the
suspected cause of the accident is a failed switch—a mechanical error. The officer confirms that one of the derailed cars is
carrying sulphuric acid and another contains an ammonia
compound. According to the fire inspector, though, they pose no
immediate threat to the surrounding area, since the spill is
very small. A clean-up crew will be sent to the scene first thing
in the morning.

The paper's morning deadline is approaching fast, so Denise calls the city editor from a nearby phone booth to confirm how much space he will need to reserve for her story. He also decides to reserve room on the front page for one of Ken's photograph. It's very late now, and Denise and Ken finally head back to the newsroom.

Ken disappears quickly into the darkroom to process the film and Denise sits down at her terminal to compose the story. It is very short and she completes it in less than an hour—to save time she'd thought most of it out on the drive back into the city. She double-checks the facts in her notebook while the editor reads it over.

The story is then transferred electronically to the layout team in the composing room. They run galleys—a sort of mechanical first draft—proofread them and copy-edit them so that the articles allocated to each page fit the amount of space available.

While this is happening, the photo editor selects a print from the three rolls of film Ken had shot. The best photo is blown up to the right size and sent to the composing room where the layout people put it in place with Denise's story, now laid out on the camera-ready assembly to be photographed.

The assembly is photographed and plates are produced that will be attached to the presses. Then the presses are ready to roll: they must meet the early morning deadline. Thousands of copies of the newspaper—complete with Denise's story and Ken's photograph—are folded and bundled, ready to be trucked to distribution points around the city. Individual operators pick up their bundles, send some to newsstands and some to newspaper carriers for home delivery.

All over the city people open up the paper in the morning to see Denise and Ken's story on page one. The middle-of-the-night train derailment has become "news."

Responding

1. As you followed "The Story of a Story," did you become interested in the possibility of working as a reporter or a photographer? Why or why not?
2. What do you think motivates people like Denise and Ken to do a job which requires working night shifts and rushing to scenes of accidents and disasters?

FOCUS ON COLLABORATIVE LEARNING

Writing a News Story

Reporters often write a story from an angle and often the angle has to do with the point of view or bias of someone involved with the story. Arrange to work with a partner or small group with this task. Choose a leader, a recorder and a reporter.

1. Plan and write the story you think Denise would have submitted if she had seen the incident from the point of view of one of the following:

   • a train official
   • the fire inspector
   • the police officer
   • the mayor of the city

2. Have your reporter read your group's version to the class and compare it with other versions written from different points of view.

Extending

1. Suggest that your teacher arrange a field trip to a local newspaper plant and the newsroom to see it in operation and talk to some of the news personnel.
2. Arrange for a panel of news reporters to speak to your class about

   • stories they have covered,
   • the training they received,
   • the skills they need.

3. Do we receive good coverage of local, national and international stories on news broadcasts in our area? What could be done to improve the coverage? Discuss with a small group of other students.

Journalist

CAREERS IN THE MEDIA

Kathy Stunden-Hall

Curiosity Creates Challenge

Hardly anyone goes into journalism for the money. This isn't to say they lack ambition...finding a job in newspapers, magazines, television and radio and public relations is a tough job.

Armed with a bachelor of journalism from King's College, University of Nova Scotia, and a degree in French and linguistics, Alida Minchella sent resumes everywhere and knocked on several doors to find that first job. She hoped some weekly newspaper would hire her. Virtually everyone has to start small and it's usually to their advantage because they gain a broader experience working for a smaller company.

Minchella got a job with a small city daily newspaper working as a reporter, taking her own photographs.

She says most of her classmates had a good sense of who they were and what they wanted. Most are willing to make sacrifices to pursue their careers: weekend work, split shifts, overtime hours without pay. And the regular salary can be downright dismal.

So what attracts Alida Minchella to journalism? Curiosity, plus an insatiable desire to learn something new every day.

Public Relations

Giving the Corporate Word

Susan Caiger-Watson has the job of getting the facts out to the public. But she isn't employed by media at all. She works for one of the largest corporations in Canada...Ontario Hydro. Assistant corporate relations officer for Hydro's western regional office in London, ON, Caiger-Watson is officially in the public relations (PR) field, but uses many of the same skills as a journalist.

A corporate relations officer has to be able to communicate well, verbally and in writing. She has to be able to research since the information she conveys must be accurate.

As well as putting forward Hydro's best face, Caiger-Watson must inform the public on everything from how Hydro proposes to secure Ontario's future power supply, to dealing with PCBs, a carcinogenic chemical once used in Hydro transformers.

Corporate and internal relations are growing fields because companies are anxious to have good corporate images, both outside and to their employees. Staff members like Caiger-Watson help out internally, too. She's responsible for completing regular employees' newsletters.

Those working in the PR field often take English or journalism as a university major. Caiger-Watson studied PR at university, and several of her courses were the same as a journalist would study. She has a bachelor of public relations degree from Mount St. Vincent University in Halifax, and a degree in Canadian Studies from York University's Glendon College.

Her first degree led her into work in the business field, then back to school for a career switch and the second degree. The broader education and job experience has been a bonus in her present position, she says.

Skills demanded of her included ability to communicate, dealing with people, the ability to understand people and handle them with tact and sensitivity.

For the public relations specialist, there are lots of opportunities, working for hospitals, utilities, government, private industry, pharmaceutical companies, auto parts manufacturers.

Researcher

A Fact-finding Mission

What's an interviewer's biggest nightmare? Getting a string of yes and no answers. On CBC Radio's *Gabereau,* this never happens.

Sheila Peacock gets Vicki Gabereau's guests fired up.

True, Gabereau's folksy banter and hearty chuckles encourage guests on the weekday talk show, but researcher Peacock finds out what makes them talk before their words are transmitted across the country on Gabereau.

"I find out what gets them going, what gets them lively," says Peacock, twenty-five, who does pre-interviews with guests before they talk with the chipper Gabereau. This helps the host determine what questions will produce a lively interview. She thrilled Phil Collins by coming up with questions he hadn't been asked before, letting him chat about his favourite music.

Finding guests ranging from Collins to Mr. Potatohead, the owner of a museum dedicated to the spud, is the challenger of five staff members, including Peacock. She scans magazines and newspapers in search of guests. She even asks friends who they think would be interesting personalities for the show. Peacock also writes and edits scripts for Gabereau. While journalism training is usually required for this job,

Sheila Peacock (left) *with Vicki Gabereau.*

the ambitious Peacock proves hard workers definitely get noticed. She started working in CBC's sales and marketing department after high school. She took all the seminars going and got as much experience as possible.

She then began working at CBC-TV Vancouver's regional newsroom. Gabereau was scheduled to appear on TV and she and Gabereau got on so well that the hostess wanted Peacock on her team.

Peacock uses her experience in public relations and sales, and has learned how to sell herself. "The outgoing people really win all the time. No one wants to waste time firing you up," says Peacock.

Music Veejay

Erica Ehm Hits the Airwaves

A lot of moxy, plenty of hard work and being there when opportunity knocked are the reason that a farm girl from Quebec is one of the country's top veejays.

Erica Ehm grew up loving music, like most teenagers, ran a school spirit contest for a Montreal radio station and ended up volunteering for the radio station as a DJ at night for which she was paid in records and tapes. She worked in record stores during the day and did a cable television show at night, and when she finished high school (and several dramatic efforts) in Hudson, QU, she headed for the University of Ottawa for a degree in communications. Her interest in music continued in Ottawa where she worked as a waitress and also as a DJ.

"I always wanted to act, I wanted to be a fly on the wall in a band's life to see how they have the magic to make music. I've always been a backstage person, finding out about things," says Ehm, whose role with Much Music's successful TV video show has her front and centre several hours a week.

Her move to Toronto prompted an application to City TV through Moses Znaimer. She recalls the interview didn't go too well, but she mustered up her courage, went back in to see the boss again, and ended up answering phones in the brand new music office. Soon she was booking shoots for the entertainment show.

"I learned a lot. Then we got our licence for Much Music. I'd worked for Maclean Hunter Cable doing an entertainment show on nights and weekends. I made a demo tape and showed it to the top Veejay at Much Music. He helped me do a new demo tape and I got the job.

"I really had no experience. I had to go on live national television," she recalls. "They just threw me into it and expected me to grow up with it. My first day on the air, my jaw locked," she laughs.

What makes Erica so popular today? "I talk to people, not at them. When I first started, kids said, 'I love it when you make mistakes.'"

"I'm torn now between making a mark on the world—ultimately you live and die—I'd like to help people with the 'fame' I have. I'm still looking for the niche that I'm really good at. This is a good job, but it's a young job," she says realistically.

So, even though she's well occupied with Much Music, Erica Ehm continues to build her base of experience for the future. She writes a regular fashion column for a Toronto newspaper, designs her own line of hats, works as TG's Music Editor on a freelance basis and sees herself as a role model.

Reporter

Having a Social Impact

An elderly woman in a small Alberta community has sole care of her visually- and hearing-impaired daughter. It's getting her down and she feels she has no place to turn. She calls the CNIB (Canadian National Institute for the Blind) for help.

They contact Stephen Snelgrove at the *Barrhead Leader.* Snelgrove is editor of the weekly newspaper, read by 5200 people. He's also photographer, reporter and, at times like this, a bit of a social worker.

Snelgrove is eager to come to this woman's aid. He writes a story about her plight, appealing to others in the community to volunteer their time. A few people offer to take the daughter on one- or two-hour outings to give the mother a break.

Snelgrove likes helping people. In fact, he likes people period. As editor of Barrhead's paper, he feels a responsibility to everyone in the community.

"I like the responsibility of the job; you're like a watchdog," says Snelgrove. He covers everything in the Barrhead area, major news stories, entertainment, sports. He's not the stereotype reporter out to expose crime and corruption (who is, in reality?) He simply wants to inform the people in his community about what's happening.

It's common for him to work fifty or sixty hours a week. There's just one other reporter at the *Leader*, so they both have to work until everything's covered. Long hours are the norm since twenty-four-year-old Snelgrove began working for newspapers four years ago. When he was at the *Athabasca Advocate,* one of four papers in his current chain, he did the ad layouts, sold ads, typed copy, took the pictures, developed the pictures. Because he's had so much experience, his range of future options is wide open. He may even start his own newspaper or join a daily.

A graduate of Southern Alberta Institute of Technology's journalism program, Snelgrove advises budding newspaper reporters to get as much practice as possible before going after that first job.

"Write, write, write," he says. Basic writing skills, spelling and good grammar count a lot when Snelgrove hires a reporter now. A good attitude and enthusiasm are high on the list, too. As with most beginners, those working on papers like Snelgrove's have to be prepared for long hours and low salaries.

When he's a little tired of it all, sometimes Snelgrove thinks about getting a nine-to-five job. But then the Tuesday paper turns out really well and he's ready to sacrifice leisure time and his sleep, once again.

This material courtesy of TG Magazine, 202 Cleveland St., Toronto, ON, M4S 2W6.

Managing Editor

Maintaining a Sense of Community

David Ikeda has been described as a "meeting looking for a place to happen." Every month he sits down, telephones the members of the editorial collective of the *Nikkei Voice* and sets up an editorial meeting. Then he starts calling all over the country to find out what articles, letters and opinion pieces will be arriving from the volunteer journalists. And so begins the process that will result in another monthly issue of a newspaper that reaches thirteen thousand homes in Canada and some parts of the United States, Britain and Japan.

The *Nikkei Voice* is a volunteer-based newspaper for Japanese Canadians (*nikkei* mean a person of Japanese descent living outside Japan). As managing editor, David and his counterpart for the Japanese-language section of the paper are the only people who receive payment for their work—little payment for a lot of work. The two managing editors supervise a group of hard-working volunteers who write, edit, format and produce the ten English and six Japanese pages every month. David, who has a degree in psychology and who had no previous experience in the media, says, "I rely heavily on the expertise of my volunteers."

So how did a person so new to journalism land the position of managing editor? "The position needed filling and I was there and willing to commit to it," explains David. He retains his "day job"

selling real estate because it allows him flexibility of time, making possible his involvement in the Japanese Canadian community. At twenty-eight, David has already proven that such involvement is in his blood. As well as editing the paper, he sits on the board of directors of the Japanese Canadian Cultural Centre; he volunteers at the Japanese Buddhist Church and the Japanese United Church of Toronto; and he has raised funds for the Momiji (maple leaf) Association which helps elderly Japanese Canadians. David's experience with people and his understanding of psychology come into play as he deals with the disagreements that inevitably surface when dedicated individuals work together. "I see my function as managing more that editing," he says.

It was being sent by the *Nikkei Voice* to a Youth Conference that really hooked David. He speaks of how exciting it was to report on and how inspiring it was to see people younger than himself "really doing something."

David states that the mandate of the *Nikkei Voice* is "to create and maintain a sense of community, to establish a Japanese Canadian identity—to keep up with the communication network and what's going on, to explore some opinion, some controversy." It is clear that, as managing editor, David Ikeda's goal and that of the newspaper are inseparable.

—*Kat Mototsune*

Responding

1. What do you think is the most important characteristic of a journalist?
2. Why do you think Alida Minchella would say that working as a veejay is a "young job"?
3. What changes do you think Stephen Snelgrove would notice in his work if he moved to a city paper as a reporter?
4. What do you think motivates David Ikeda to work so hard with little pay on The *Nikkei Voice?*

FOCUS ON MEDIA LITERACY

Working in the Media

Suppose you were considering a career in the media and wanted to take stock of what you knew about the training of journalists and the work they do. Make notes about what you learned from reading the profiles of Stephen Snelgrove and David Ikeda.

- training
- working to develop a career
- pay
- intangible rewards
- importance of being versatile
- basic skills
- role of human relations
- making a commitment

Extending

1. Research a media role you are interested in. You may be able to obtain information by

   - visiting a counsellor,
   - writing to a school of journalism,
   - talking to a journalist.

2. Get together with a group of other students to write a class newspaper for a short period of time. Organize yourselves to play the different roles involved (editor, reporters, printers, etc.).

   Cover events in your class and in the school as a whole and distribute copies to other classes.

MEMORABLE
SPORTS PHOTOS

American tennis champion John McEnroe became famous for his public outbursts of bad temper. (Opposite page)

America's Jesse Owens (centre) *stands on the podium before receiving the gold medal for broad jump in the 1936 Olympics held in Germany. Lutz Long, the German silver medallist* (right), *gives a Nazi salute. During the medal-awarding ceremony, Hitler refused to shake hands with the black athlete.*

Britain's Jayne Torvill and Christopher Dean, Olympic gold medallists, practise their ice dance routines (opposite page, top left).

Tears stream down the cheeks of the U.S. runner Valerie Brisco-Hooks as she listens to the American national anthem during the 1984 Olympics, in which she won the gold medal for women's 200 metres (opposite page, top right).

American sprinter Mary Decker bounces off the grass tripped by Britain's Zola Budd during the 1984 Olympic Games (opposite page, bottom).

Teen Soviet gymnast Olga Korbut (above right) *performs on the balance beam.*

Wayne Gretzky hugs a Los Angeles Kings teammate after breaking Gordie Howe's NHL career points record in Edmonton in 1989.

Responding

1. Which picture(s) are the best action shots? What skills or techniques did they freeze for the viewer?
2. Which pictures tell a story? Reconstruct the sequence of events.
3. Which picture(s) make a political statement? What do they say about people and ideas?

FOCUS ON VISUAL REPRESENTATION

Preparing for a Photo Shoot

Imagine that you are a staff photographer for a newspaper and your editor sends you to cover a major sporting event. Your responsibility is to produce the pictures for a full-page photo spread on the event. Make a working plan for the shoot.

- What is the event? Rehearse the program in advance. In what order will things happen? What interesting people will be there? Where will you position yourself for good photos?
- Make a detailed plan listing the pictures you will attempt to shoot. Remember that good photographers take many pictures to ensure a good selection.
- Make rough sketches of some of the pictures you plan to take so that you'll know in advance how you plan to frame them.
- Take a large sheet of newsprint and rough out design for the full-page spread.

Extending

1. Find out as much as you can about the training regimen of successful athletes in various sports. What training routines do they follow? According to what basic principles are the routines designed? How do the various routines differ from one another and what features do they have in common?
2. Collect as many sports photos as you can from sports magazines and sources such as *Life.* Share them with other students and choose the best for a classroom display, grouping them according to themes.

NEW PLACES, NEW FACES

Canada has historicallly welcomed immigrants, and this is still true—nearly 40 per cent of Toronto's population, 30 per cent of Vancouver's and 20 per cent of Edmonton's and Calgary's were foreign-born.

The streets on the Monopoly board are named after streets of Atlantic City. The three most landed-on spaces are Illinois Avenue, Go and B&O railroad.

Pidgin is a language which two groups of people develop to use in common. In the 17th century, British traders spoke to their Chinese customers in a combination of English and Chinese which became known as "pidgin"—a Cantonese version of the English word "business."

THE MYSTERY OF THE FRANKLIN EXPEDITION

Elizabeth MacLeod

John Torrington. You many not know the name but you probably know his face. With clenched teeth and empty blue eyes, he stares out through a hundred and forty years of Arctic snow and ice, looking almost the same as he did when he was buried on January 1, 1846.

Torrington's grave on Beechey Island in the Northwest Territories was the first of a group of three that was investigated by a team of scientists based at the University of Alberta in Edmonton. From 1981 to 1986, these experts spent their summers in Canada's far north, searching for clues to the mystery surrounding an expedition of British sailors who all died there between 1846 and 1848. By examining the bodies of the three seamen, the scientists hoped to discover the reason why the Franklin Expedition ended in tragedy without a single survivor.

The Franklin Expedition was led by Sir John Franklin, a British sea captain who had sailed all over the world and had been to the Arctic a number of times. For hundreds of years, sailors had been searching for a route over the top of North America to China. If if existed, it would mean a much faster way to the silk, spices and other treasures of the Far East. By the time Sir John sailed on this fatal voyage, China was already very accessible through warmer waters, but the desire to be the first to find the Northwest Passage was still strong.

So Franklin set out with the two ships, the HMS *Erebus* and the HMS *Terror,* both well equipped with food, such as sacks of flour, cans of preserved meats and vegetables and other necessities including a music organ for each ship, mahogany writing desks and that new invention, the camera. The ships also carried lemon juice to prevent scurvy, a disease caused by a lack of vitamin C in the diet.

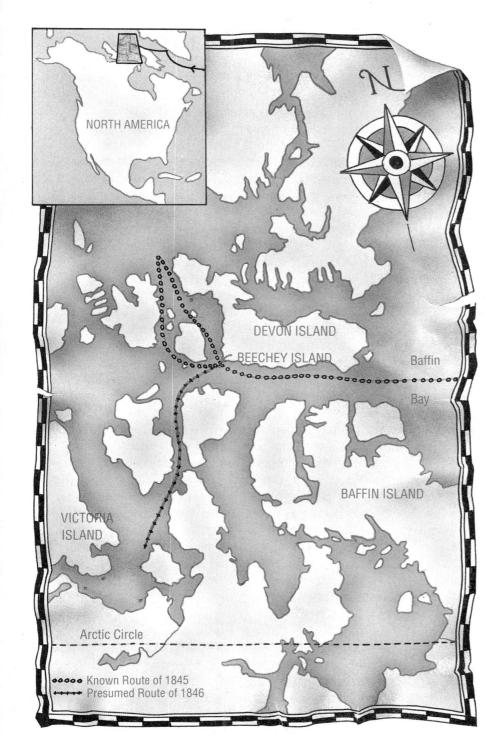

NORTH AMERICA

N

DEVON ISLAND

BEECHEY ISLAND

Baffin

Bay

BAFFIN ISLAND

VICTORIA
ISLAND

Arctic Circle

ooooo Known Route of 1845
++++ Presumed Route of 1846

The last contact the men of the Franklin Expedition had with their friends and family was in August 1845 when they left Greenland. After that, the little information we have about where they went and how they died is only what was gathered by the many expeditions that went in search of the missing sailors. Franklin had taken enough food to last his men five or possibly seven years since he knew they would spend a number of winters frozen motionless in the thick Arctic ice. So, although the first searchers had hopes of finding the sailors alive, those hopes soon dwindled. Franklin's wife, Lady Jane Franklin, convinced the British government to send a number of expeditions and even raised money herself to finance a ship to search for traces of her husband.

However, the searchers found very little. Some relics (such as buttons, cans, glassware, etc.), a number of monuments erected by the crew and containing scraps of information, a few skeletons, and the three graves on Beechey Island was all that was left. Although twenty-five expeditions searched for the crewmen, not a trace was found of the ships or any records to tell them how the 129 men died. It wasn't until 1982 that there was a breakthrough in the mystery surrounding the tragic expedition.

In the summer of 1981, a team from the University of Alberta led by anthropologist Owen Beattie arrived on King William Island in the Northwest Territories. By carefully studying the accounts of an 1878 expedition that had searched for Franklin, the team knew where they were most likely to find relics and other clues to the mystery. It was dangerous, exhausting work since the group had to carry all their equipment and food over melting ice and massive drifts of snow. The threat of polar bear attack was constant. However, in an area scattered with a few artefacts (including parts of a clay pipe) that would have been used at the time of the Franklin Expedition, they found fragments of a skull and other bones. Because of the artefacts, and because the bones were so weathered and pitted, they were able to determine that the bones were from the same time period as the Expedition. By examining the skull, they could also tell that it was Caucasian and male. It was safe to assume that the bones belonged to one of the long-dead sailors.

Back in Edmonton, the scientists spent the next winter analyzing their finds. Marks on the bones indicated that the starving men had probably resorted to cannibalism in an effort to stay alive. What was more amazing was the amount of lead found in the bones: about ten times the level found in bones from the same era! And it wasn't difficult to figure out where that lead came from. Not only was much of the Franklin Expedition's food in lead-sealed cans, but they also used

A Victorian search party discovers the remains of one of Franklin's sailors.

lead-glazed pottery and tableware. However, only if Beattie and his team could examine actual body tissue of one of the dead crewmen, could they discover if the lead poisoning definitely had occurred before the men set sail or during the expedition. Those graves on Beechey Island might hold the final clue.

It was difficult getting permission to dig up the graves and many government departments in both Canada and Britain had to be contacted. Beattie even had to place an ad in The *Times* newspaper in London requesting that any descendants of the three Franklin crewmen get in touch with him to give him permission for his proposed work. (He got no response.) But Beattie was gambling on the hope that the ice and freezing temperatures of those cold graves would have preserved the bodies well enough that there would still be tissue he could analyze.

The scientists decided to exhume Petty Officer John Torrington first. The grave had to be carefully sketched and photographed so that they could leave it in exactly the same state in which they'd found it. Stones were even numbered to help the team put them back in the right place. Then they erected a tent over the site for protection and set to work digging through the permafrost.

Using pick and shovel, it took the men two days just to get through 1.5 metres of the permanently frozen ground. It was slow, back-breaking work, so when one of the men yelled "That's it! We've got it!" and they all knew they had finally reached Torrington's coffin, there was a huge sense of relief.

At this point, the investigation was faced with a major emergency. Rain, sleet and melting snow began to run into the grave and threatened to damage the coffin and its contents. The crew quickly had to dig a ditch to direct the water away from the grave and the situation was saved. But the rain storms got worse and as the men got closer and closer to completely uncovering the coffin lid, thunder crashed and winds howled. "This is like something out of a horror film," thought one of the men. The wind actually lifted the tent and almost carried it away but luckily there was no damage to the gravesite.

When Beattie's team finally got the coffin open, they found a huge block of ice and were immediately faced with the problem of how to melt it without damaging the body. Buckets of hot and cold water seemed to work best but the stench of decaying wool was incredible. However, the men continued, working from the feet up, and were amazed at how well preserved the body was. Gently they pulled back the cloth covering Torrington's face and suddenly he gazed out at them. His nose and forehead were darkened from having the dark blue cloth lying on them, but otherwise his colour was quite normal. The hard-working scientists knew it was a moment they would never forget.

The body was examined, samples taken and then the coffin was reburied. The summer was almost over and the men would have to return to examine the graves of the two other men, Able Seaman John Hartnell and Private William Braine.

When the last two graves were examined during the summer of 1986 there were many things that were different from the previous examination. The scientists already knew that Hartnell's grave had been disturbed at some point after he had been buried and that it was much closer to the surface than Torrington's had been. They weren't prepared for the amount of decomposition that had already occurred in Braine's body, indicating that it may have been some time after he died before he was buried. Something else that was different about that summer's investigation was that the men were joined by a descendant of Hartnell's, Brian Spencely, who was the group's official photographer. Imagine what it must have been like for him to look into the eyes of an ancestor who had been dead for more than a century.

When tissue from the three bodies was examined, it was found that lead-poisoning had contributed to the deaths of all three men. By analyzing hair samples taken, experts could determine exactly when the poisoning had taken place and it was definitely found to be during the time of the Franklin Expedition. Canned food, even today, can be contaminated with lead because of the lead solder used to seal and seam cans, and when Beattie examined cans used by the tragic expedition he found many of the seams were faulty and could have easily resulted in poisoning.

Another interesting part of the scientific analysis of the material that Beattie and this team brought back was the attempt to culture, or breed, bacteria from the dead men in order to identify the organisms. Because of this, bacteria dating back to 1864 and once living in William Braine are alive today.

The Franklin Expedition is a remarkable story of courage and suffering. Thanks to the efforts of modern-day explorers we have been given a glimpse of what the men endured and have gained an understanding of a mystery that has amazed the world for almost a hundred and fifty years.

(Reference source, *Frozen in Time* by Owen Beattie and John Geiger, Western Producer Prairie Books)

Responding

1. The article mentions that you have probably seen John Torrington's face before. Where might you have seen it?
2. Why was the quest for the Northwest Passage so important to Europe in the past?
3. How did Beattie's team know where to look for the relics of the Franklin Expedition?
4. What do you think you would have experienced if you had been present at an exhumation?

FOCUS ON DRAMA

Dramatizing an Incident

Work together with a group of your classmates to dramatize the incident in the article in which John Torrington's coffin is dug up.

- Write a short narrative about the incident, with beginning, complications, climax and ending.
- Decide what the characters should be like to make for interesting conflict within the research team.
- Visualize what the stage should look like. What will you choose as the setting? How will you let the audience know that the broad setting is the Arctic? How will you show the time of year and time of day?
- Plan the script, complete with actors' lines and stage directions.
- Divide the following roles among the members of your group: actors, director, props attendant.
- Practise the scene and present it to your class.

Extending

1. The search for the Franklin Expedition has given rise to much creative activity. Try to locate and read or view some of the accounts.
2. Compose an advertisement for a British newspaper, saying that you plan to dig up the grave of John Torrington, why you wish to do so and ask for permission from any living relatives. Strive for a good balance between keeping the message brief enough for a good advertisement and detailed enough so that all essential information is included.
3. Imagine that you are a member of the expedition which completed the exhumation of the Torrington gravesite. Write a letter to your family about the experience.

In the mid 1920s, the northern part of Canada was still very much a developing country with few communities, few roads and even fewer schoolhouses. In Northern Ontario there were many children of prospectors, trappers and railway workers who were getting no education at all because of this. That's when the government of Ontario came up with a plan in cooperation with the three railroads. If the railroads would supply some cars, the government would fit them out as rolling schoolrooms, complete with teachers. These school cars would be able to go wherever the rails could take them, which was just about anywhere there were people, and the children could attend a unique kind of one-room school. The plan worked; and it was in these moving classrooms that many northern children received an education. Eighty-one-year-old Florence Bell says she remembers all of her students, as well as some of the great characters who lived in isolation beside the railroad track.

THE SCHOOL CARS OF ONTARIO

Florence Bell

The war was still on when my husband and I, along with our two children, took that job. We were the only husband-and-wife team of teachers—that is to say, where both of us actually taught. He would be teaching some students up at one end of the classroom, and I'd be teaching others down at the other end. The classroom was one half of the railcar, and in the other half we had our living quarters which had all the comforts of a regular home. Two bedrooms, a living room, kitchen and bathroom. It was very nice really, and there were very few problems except for one winter when we had trouble with heat. Now, in a country where the temperature outside gets down to minus thirty-seven degrees Celsius, that could be very serious but someone came and fixed that up before we froze to death.

When we first took that posting, I was full of misgivings. After all, what was it going to be like living day in day out on a railroad car, half of which was a schoolroom, parked on a railroad siding? I wondered how we would get any sense of permanence when we would never be in one location any longer than a week. How would we ever get to know any neighbours, and how would our children ever get to have any permanent friends? These were only a few of the doubts I had, but do you know, these fears were all groundless.

Right from the very first day we loved it. When we went to bed we could hear the sound of a nearby waterfall, the roar of the rapids in the river and the tiny noises coming from the forest that never stop. We slept soundly the first night and after a good breakfast in the morning we sat there and waited for our new students to show up.

The first who came were a boy and a girl from a Finnish family, a couple of tiny tots. Next, from across the tracks, came a little Norwegian-French girl, a beautiful little blonde. Her cousins from Sudbury were staying with them at the time, and they also came. The Pratt

A school-car lesson in progress. Most of the children had never had the opportunity to attend school before.

children showed next. Their father was English and their mother was Cree, and they told us two things: their father drank beer, and if you tell lies you don't go to heaven.

Our two children stood there looking at these children shyly and the new children just as shyly looked at them. After lunch the children came back to school with two kittens and a pup which they gave to my two. Then they were friends.

At the end of our first day we gave the children homework, and we went to our living quarters and wondered if what we were doing would have any kind of an impact on these children and their fami-

lies. What would they think of us? Intruders in their midst. Well, we didn't have long to wait. The Finnish family sent over an invitation to us to have a sauna in the little log cabin they had built for that purpose. It was a unique experience for me, as I had never even heard the word "sauna" before. Afterwards, we went up to their house for coffee. We didn't speak Finnish, and they didn't speak English, but we managed to have a great time anyway.

When we left after a week, we left five weeks of homework for the children to complete before we returned again. When the engine came to pull our car away to the next community my only thoughts were, "Will they do it? Will they be able to do the homework by themselves?" You see, many of the parents had no education at all, and therefore wouldn't be able to help them.

What I really loved about those four years in our moving one-room school was the wonderful people. They were really exceptional, and so anxious to learn that we never had discipline problems of any sort. We never had parents complain either. Homework was always done, and you must remember when I mention homework, I mean *a lot* of it. We would only be in each place for a week before we moved on to the next for a week, and then on to another and another. They always had it finished when we came back.

When we first started, we only had nineteen children between all the stops on the whole line where our school car went. At some stops we'd have only one or two, but at others there would be seven or eight. Those numbers grew as time went on, and by the time we left, we had a total of sixty on that line. There were seven different cars on seven different lines, so a lot of northern children got their education that way.

Most of the children who came to classes had never before been to school, and it was such a delight to see the way they took to it. You could see those minds just expanding day by day. They were like sponges soaking it all up. We taught in English, of course, but we were dealing with children who spoke twenty-eight different languages between them, as the North was full of new immigrants in those days. Even though they didn't speak English, however, they had no trouble understanding. In his report on our students at the end of the year the school inspector said, "They are better than my best rural school and as good as my best urban school." One of my students who had to leave during her grade ten year because her father was moving to the city led her new class in Latin in that city. They all were such very good students.

Like the others, our car was beautifully equipped and furnished. The CPR paid for the furnishings and the department of education in Ontario supplied all the books and other equipment, so in reality we were much better off than most of the traditional one-room schools.

My own children were better off, too, because of it. They had good friends at every stop, and they were enriched by the experience of knowing children of so many nationalities. They skied, skated, and canoed, and were never bored or asking, "What will we do today?" as so many city children do. Our living quarters were really modern for the times. We had proper beds, an up-to-date kitchen and the bathroom even had a tub, which you don't often see on a train. The only pioneering aspect of life for me was going down to the lake in winter, breaking the ice and carrying the water back to heat it on the coal-burning kitchen stove so I could do the weekly wash.

When we were at a location, the parents all came down to the school on Friday nights for a social evening. We had a movie projector, and they really enjoyed that. I remember one man saying, "It's the first time I saw a moving picture in twenty years." You see, most

On snowshoes and skis, the students turn up for their classes in the depth of winter.

Another thing, too, was the wildlife. It was not unusual at all to look out the classroom window and see a big moose or a bear looking back at you. The kids loved that, and these were about the only times I had trouble getting them to pay attention to their studies. There were a lot of black bears up there, and the kids would make a game of it—who will see the first bear today? Nobody, least of all the children, seemed to have any fear of them. They never came too near, and of course we never, never went too near to them. It seemed that whenever you went outside to pick berries there was always a bear off somewhere in the background, watching us, just as we were watching them.

Altogether there were seven of these school cars in Ontario, each one serving a different part of the north. It was the only such system in the world, and it was perfectly suited for the terrain and the times. Later on, Brazil patterned a system after ours, as did Mexico. Newfoundland also put in a system. The state of Arizona in the U.S. also sent people up here to look at ours before they went back to start a school-car system of their own. But ours was the very first, and, I like to think, the best!

Gradually, as the North began filling up with more people, and more permanent communities were established with their own schools, the need for the school cars died out. It was in the mid-sixties before the last one closed, though.

It was a terrific thing to have been involved in, and I must say that my four years in them were probably the best years of my life.

of them had left the cities and towns of the south for a different kind of life—hunting, trapping, fishing and lumbering, and so on—and so even an ordinary movie in a made-over railroad car was a real treat.

They showered us with apple pies and cakes and all kinds of other good things. Those Friday-night gatherings were really special to them and equally special to us. For some of the women, it would be their only night out until the school car came around again in six weeks' time. When we came around again into the community after such a long time away, everybody was there to greet us and welcome us back like long-lost friends. They'd all be there, parents and children, crowding around the railroad siding, waiting for the car to come to a stop. You couldn't help feeling so welcome—eyes would be shining, everyone smiling and waving and every stop was like that.

Responding

1. What kind of person would enjoy the kind of life depicted in the article?
2. Would you have enjoyed this kind of schooling? Why or why not?
3. Why do you think the children who were taught in the school cars were so curious and anxious to learn? Is this in any way a comment on traditional schooling?
4. What was the impact of life in the school car on the author's children?

FOCUS ON WRITING

Writing a Report

Imagine that you are a school inspector working for the Ministry of Education. This is the first year, an experimental time for the school cars. Your job is to write a report for the ministry to assist with the decision whether to give the school cars permanent status.

- What details would you provide about
  - the curriculum?
  - the quality of the cars and equipment?
  - the attitudes of the students and the progress they are making?
  - the qualifications and suitability of the teachers?
  - the comments of the parents?
- What recommendations will you make about improving the experience for the students?
- What will you say in your overall recommendation whether to make the school cars permanent?

Extending

1. Write a short narrative depicting a morning in a school car from a student's point of view. Think about

   - how the setting will look,
   - who your characters will be,
   - the subjects to be taken,
   - the events which will occur.

2. Get together with a partner to compare your school experiences today with those of the young people who attended the school cars. What similarities did you note? What differences? Did you conclude that the similarities or the differences were the more striking?

SHANAWDITHIT THE LAST OF THE BEOTHUK

Lauren Wolk

In 1610, when English seaman John Guy founded the first recorded white settlement in Newfoundland, he feasted and traded peacefully with the native Beothuk and arranged to hold a second exchange of goods the following year. But the next season, when another ship happened to come across the large assembly of Beothuk waiting for Guy to keep his appointment, the captain fired his cannon into the crowd, thinking they were hostile. From that day on, all contact with white settlers proved to be disastrous to the Beothuk.

War, disease and European settlement took a heavy toll, and by the spring of 1823, only a handful of Beothuk remained. Forced from their winter hunting grounds, they waited desperately for the warm weather to arrive and, in the meantime, starved. Their only hope for survival was the sea, which had always made their summers plentiful. If they managed to reach the shore and if ice melted in time, they had a chance. But the Beothuk were constantly threatened by trappers who murdered in cold blood or took captives for exhibition and enslavement. And tuberculosis, the "coughing demon" that had devastated their tribe and already infected several of the survivors, was an equally potent enemy.

Just before reaching the shore they ran into a group of furriers— most of the Beothuk party were killed. Two young women managed to hide, but their mother, Doodebewshet, was captured. Knowing that her daughters would die of starvation, Doodebewshet led her captors to their hiding place.

The three Beothuk women were taken to St John's, Newfoundland. Like other captives before them, Doodebewshet and her daughters were dressed in European garb in an effort to transform them into

A nineteenth-century portrait of Shanawdithit.

Christian servants. Before long, however, Newfoundland's governor decided that they should be set free to search for any other Beothuk survivors. And so they were sent back to their home.

Before long, Doodebewshet and one of her daughters died of tuberculosis, leaving the remaining daughter completely alone. Her name was Shanawdithit. Her way of life destroyed and her people gone, Shanawdithit's only chance for survival was to return to white society and live among those who had made her the last surviving Beothuk.

After working for several years as a servant in a Twillingate household, Shanawdithit was sent to St. John's in 1827 to live with William Epps Cormack, an explorer, naturalist and scholar. He had become interested in the Beothuk, founded the Beothuk Institute to advocate their protection and conducted an unsuccessful expedition to locate survivors. To Cormack, Shawnadithit represented the last chance to preserve something of her culture.

Shanawdithit did her best to teach him about her people, their customs and their religious beliefs. But she was also an artist whose drawings vividly depicted the lost way of life of the Beothuk. She drew ceremonial objects and explained their significance. She drew pictures of food, shelters, clothing and people. She gave form to the Beothuk concept of evil. She made maps and annotated them with descriptions of incidents that had occurred before the Beothuk had been forced to flee from their ancestral homes. Through her art Shanawdithit spoke for her lost people.

It is remarkably sad that more is known of how the Beothuk died than of how they lived, that their extinction is one of few certainties among a great many guesses. But Shanawdithit's art is a lasting memorial to her people. It is her promise that they will not be forgotten.

Not much is known about these ceremonial staffs. Any notes beyond those that accompany Shanawdithit's drawings have been lost.

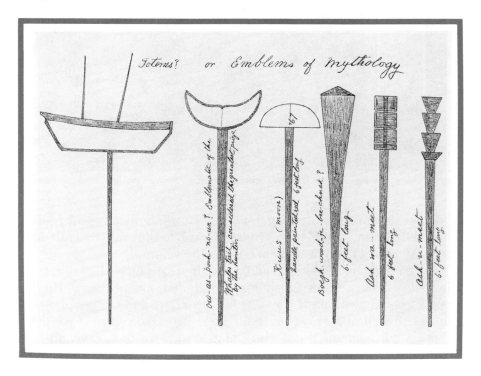

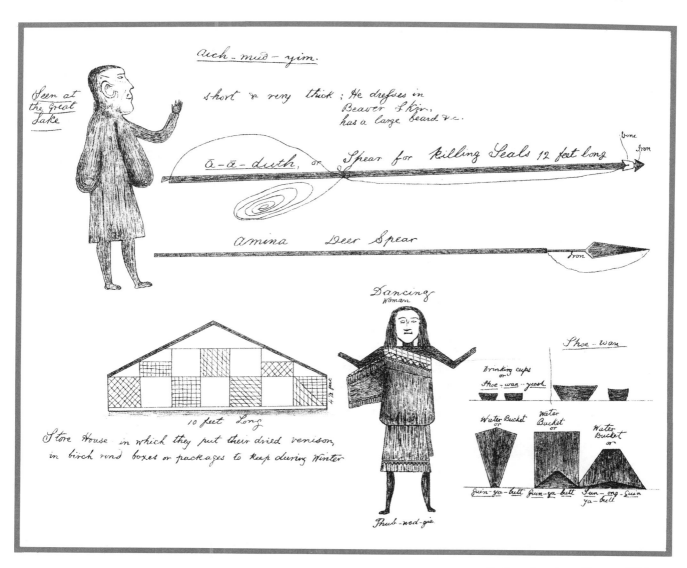

auch - mud - yim.

Seen at the Great Lake

short & very thick; He dresses in
Beaver Skin,
has a large beard &c.

ā - ā - duth, or Spear for Killing Seals 12 feet long

bone
Iron

amina   Deer Spear

Iron

Dancing Woman

Shoe - wan

Drinking cups
or
Shoe - wan - yeesh

Water Bucket
or

Water Bucket
or

Water Bucket
or

10 feet Long

Store House in which they put their dried venison,
in birch rind boxes or packages to keep during Winter

Thub - wed - gis.

Guin - ya - butt   Guin - ya - butt   Gun - ong - Guin
ya - butt

In these drawings, Shanawdithit portrayed spirits and symbols of the Beothuk religion, as well as objects of everyday use.

Responding

1. Why do you think the Beothuk became extinct?
2. How do you feel about the fact that races of people have disappeared and are still disappearing from the face of the earth? Is there any way to prevent their extinction?
3. Do you think the effort to discover what past cultures were like is worthwhile? Why or why not?
4. How do you feel about the fact that "more is known of how the Beothuk died than of how they lived"?

FOCUS ON VISUAL REPRESENTATION

Sketching Pictures

Imagine that you and your family travel to a remote island for a vacation. On the voyage, all of the other members of your family are lost at sea and you are rescued by friendly islanders with whom you have no language in common. You can tell, however, that they are interested in learning about your people and your culture.

Working together with two or three other students, sketch and colour a series of pictures to communicate with the islanders. Include pictures of

- your family and other people,
- your customs and way of life,
- your food,
- your religious beliefs,
- important events in your past,
- maps showing where you come from.

Add captions and make a display of your pictures in the school.

Extending

1. Imagine that the early settlers who brought the Beothuk to extinction are to be tried before a judge and jury. You are to be the prosecuting attorney. Make notes for the opening address you will give at the trial, laying out the evidence of the settlers' guilt.
2. Search for information about the disappearance of Native culture and Native languages. Get together with a small group and share your opinions about the causes of the disappearance of Native languages and cultures and possible remedies.

Leslie Mack-Mumford has just finished a gruelling 500-kilometre scientific/canoeing adventure along the Kazan River in the Northwest Territories with the British-based Operation Raleigh program. The following are excerpts from her daily journal. After the first week, Mack-Mumford, a recent graduate from the Ontario Science Centre School, stopped using dates before her entries because she said she wanted to see what it was like to go for weeks without knowing the day or time.

Day 2

How do I feel? I love it here...Yesterday, we found hearths and tent rings and arrowheads and flakes (stone chips from ancient tools) and a small *inuksuit* (rock structure made to resemble man to mark a path)...I was really cold last night...but the sun's still shining away...Eddie came and showed us a full rainbow.

Day 3

I still don't feel like I'm here...in the all-mighty barrenlands. All today was pretty dismal, grey and rainy and looking about was not much of a breathtaking sight. Yet tonight beauty, the realness of life. So absorbing.

Day 5

We walked and walked and walked and walked. Through bog and willow thickets, through snow and ice and scrambling over rocks, all the while keeping a lookout for birds, flowers, and of course, archaeological artefacts.

Day 6

I kissed the ground today. I was so pleased to have landed alive and dry. For the first time I realized and felt the true power of the Kazan...Andrew and I were canoeing down through the middle of the rapids when these swells came up from nowhere. They just kept growing and growing. I could not believe it. There

FOND MEMORIES OF CARIBOU, MUSKOX AND "DARN BUGS"

Leslie Mack-Mumford

Leslie Mack-Mumford (left) *relaxes before another stint of paddling along the Kazan River in the Northwest Territories.*

Leslie (left) *and other members of the Operation Raleigh adventure trip.*

was nothing, absolutely nothing, we could do. They turned us sideways and we must have been at a forty-five-degree angle before we somehow managed to right ourselves...I wanted to get out of the water. I felt unsafe, tired and cold. I was so scared. He was wonderful. Always calm and giving words of confidence, and you're doing great. Thank you, Andrew.

Now for the best part of the day. WOLVES! Real live wolves flying across the tundra. Literally flying. It looks so easy, a gentle lope across the tundra.

Day 7

Distances are something curious. The constant need to concentrate on the next footstep is so absorbing that one forgets to look ahead. Only once one has reached the destination and a moment's time is taken for reflection does one realize how far one actually has come.

I think I'm finding the "nothing" in this country of miles and miles of noth-

ing. The minute, the hidden, the unchangeable, the dramatic, the shy, the larger than life. The delicate beauty and intricacy of Arctic blossoms, the birds in their undemanding plumage, the never-ceasing flow and mosaic of the river, the winds, the rains, the sweltering heat, the gentle lope of the arctic wolf.

●●●

Yahoo! Wild rapids man! I couldn't believe it. I actually looked forward and felt confident about shooting this lot with Mike. Tons of water shoot by you and want to pull you under but you manage to evade their constant tugs. What an incredible day. I didn't even count the hours. I didn't think at all. I lived!

●●●

Today we all had the worst possible conditions combined in one: no wind, rain, uncountable millions of bugs and all this while digging an archaeological tent ring. I love excavation work and today was tremendously interesting for we actually got to see more than just the surface of a tent ring. By unearthing it, it almost felt like we were a part of it.

I couldn't be bothered to tuck my shirt into my pants and as a result—to my horror—Angela pointed out an entire line of blackfly bites along my lower back. They neither itch nor hurt when bitten—it's just gross.

•••

Another day in the barrenlands:

Look! Caribou and more and more moving like a line of beetles with funny furry antenna. After supper I went to look and enjoy. For hours we sat soaking in the excitement of the passing animals. Many females with young. George and I continued to the far hill. There we saw millions standing in the dark…you could hear their breathing and the clicking of their hooves…. And this is how I spent my birthday!

•••

Leaving the Kazan held mixed feelings.

The change in landscape—flat and sandy—was welcome, but the idea of finally leaving the mighty river was not. Not really…. The thousands of caribou, the muskox, the cotton grass—none will remember me. But I shall carry them with me wherever I go, very deep in my heart, and with fondness I will remember all but those darned bugs.

Responding

1. Locate the Kazan River on a map of the Northwest Territories. Approximately how long is it? Through what kinds of country does it flow?
2. What is the apparent purpose of the expedition in the article? How do you know?
3. Have you ever been to a remote place, perhaps on a camping trip? Find a partner and exchange stories about what happened.
4. What do you think the author means by

   • "I still don't feel like I'm here…"
   • "Distances are sometimes curious…"
   • "I think I'm finding the 'nothing' in this country…"
   • "…the birds in their undemanding plumage…"

FOCUS ON COLLABORATIVE LEARNING

Planning an Expedition

Get together with a group of four or five other students to plan an expedition to an isolated place far away. Make decisions such as the following:

- What is the destination of your choice? What attracts you to it?
- Whose permission will you need? Whom will you inform about your expedition?
- How will you raise the money to go?
- What equipment and provisions will you take with you?
- How will you get there? How will you travel during the expedition?
- What guides will you take with you? How will you judge their competence when you interview them?
- What will each member of the expedition be responsible for?

Collect pictures of the territory you would travel through and weave them into an imaginary journal of the experience.

Extending

1. Find all the information you can about Operation Raleigh.
2. With a partner, make a photo collection of Arctic wildlife, scenery and people. Display your collection in the classroom.
3. Imagine you are Leslie Mack-Mumford and write a letter to your English employer telling him or her that you have been delayed on your expedition to the Canadian North and that you will not be able to be back at work on the date promised. Provide lots of convincing detail.

ONSTAGE & OFF

In Shakespeare's day, women were not allowed to act on stage, so female parts were taken by boys.

Theatre people consider it bad luck to wish someone good luck. Instead, they wish each other to "break a leg."

Drama has its origins in ancient games and rituals. Hunters acted out the hunt to ensure success or to placate the spirit of their prey, while farmers sought the renewal of the seasons and the rains.

THE MAKING OF GANDHI

Richard Attenborough

To make a film about the life of Mahatma Gandhi is an awesome responsibility. Indians revere him as a holy man who led India to independence after centuries as a British colony. Gandhi showed us all how to achieve political change by means of non-violent—but active—civil protest, and I believe his method of peaceful protest is increasingly relevant in today's troubled world.

In 1962 Motilal Kothari, an Indian civil servant living in London, asked me to make a film about Gandhi. I read a biography and some of the Mahatma's own words before making what eventually became a twenty-year commitment to completing the film. When I began to research in India itself, I discovered that the bibliography on Gandhi is more extensive than for almost any other person except Christ. In addition, he was

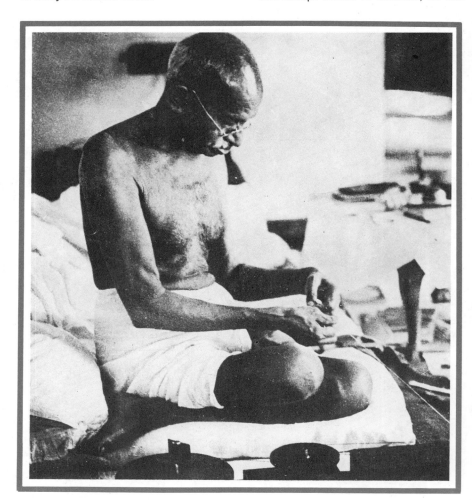

Mahatma Gandhi at the spinning wheel.

also one of the most photographed people of the twentieth century—perhaps even more so than Franklin D. Roosevelt or Winston Churchill.

My main goal in making the film was to be as faithful as possible to the spirit of the man. I wanted to discover the truth about Gandhi by studying all the available material. If, in compressing the seventy-nine years of his life into a motion picture of just over three hours' duration, I had to depart from certain historical facts, it was essential that accurate research made me aware of exactly what cinematic liberties I was taking. If I were to depart from information that was incorrect in the first place, I would be in danger of arriving at totally unacceptable decisions.

A biography is someone's opinion containing conscious or unconscious biases. A photograph is a fact—a frozen moment in time—even when you don't know all the circumstances surrounding its existence. The film, I hope, presents the visual as well as the philosophical truth about Gandhi, and the former derives largely from a vast number of historical photographs which we studied minutely.

The Gandhi National Museum in New Delhi covers two floors of a building close to Rajghat, the site of the Gandhi Memorial near the Yamuna River where Gandhi's body was cremated in 1948. Officials there were immensely cooperative in showing me their collection of photographs and in printing huge blow-ups for reference purposes. I have since discovered that almost every picture ever taken of Gandhi by people all over the world has been donated to the museum. Ironically, some of the oldest

pictures from large glass plate negatives, dating back to the last century, are of better quality than later photographs preserved on film.

All of these helped us in making *Gandhi*. Some determined the concept, set-up and composition of sequences in the film. Often we framed a scene in exactly the same position and with the same light source as the original photographer. The archive photographs showed postures, clothing, personal relationships and attitudes that helped the screenwriter, the actors and all of us to bring authenticity to various settings and characterizations.

As an actor myself, I know that lack of confidence can detrimentally inhibit a performance. When an actor walks on to a movie set, he is surrounded by people who wonder whether he will make a fool of himself or whether there will be a truth in what he is doing. Anything that can give him an insight into characterization grants him confidence. The resultant authority helps him to relax so that he can take risks, venture into giving a performance of which he was almost unaware he was capable. Historical photographs gave the actors in *Gandhi* their confidence because they could see exactly what they were aiming for visually.

Ben Kingsley, who gives a brilliant performance as Gandhi, has to depict some fifty-four years of his life. Ben, who is in his late thirties, had to go far beyond what one would assume his normal physical capabilities to be. The fact that he could look at a still and see for himself how Gandhi dressed or held his head or wore his hair gave him great assurance. As director, I could talk to

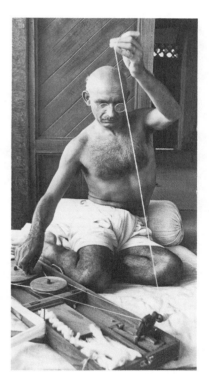

Ben Kingsley as Gandhi. The archival photos of the Mahatma helped the actor to capture Gandhi's particular gestures and expressions.

Ben for hours on end and still be unable to help him in the same way as one archive photograph.

All the actors playing historical characters, such as Gandhi's wife Kasturbai, Nehru, Patel, Kriplani and Jinnah relied on photographs to help build their characters.

The pictures of Gandhi gathering salt from the Indian Ocean beach at Dandi after his famous 390-km march provide a good example of how archive material helped to set the mood. Gandhi was a very gentle man. I have never seen a picture of him in an aggressive posture. One so often sees him with a marvellous grin on his face giving a characteristic little wave of his hand. We framed the scene of Ben picking up salt exactly as it was in the photo. He positioned his feet and hands in just the same way that Gandhi did. He even held the salt high above his head—emulating perfectly the one defiant gesture of the Mahatma's life—as he claimed it as the birthright of the Indian people.

Every department on the film—props, wardrobe, set construction—used massive files of stills. The makeup for each character had to be carefully worked out before we went into production. Once we started shooting there was no time to improvise. To play Gandhi in his seventies, Ben had to be in the makeup chair at 5:30 a.m. in order to appear on the set by 9:30 a.m.

It was not easy to show characters in different stages of ageing over the fifty-four years covered by the film. At some periods in his life Gandhi shaves his whole head, at others only part of it. Now and then he let his hair grow on the sides. Only the archive pictures demon-strated this clearly and factually. If we had followed an apparently logical process of ageing without recourse to them, the movie could necessarily have been predictable. But, captured in the photographs, Gandhi might look at a particular time very elderly and frail. Two years later he would seem comparatively young again, just as all of us probably go through such changes in appearance due to ill health, diet and prevailing circumstances.

Gandhi's teeth were important in indicating his age as gradually they fell out or were extracted until finally he wore false ones. He used seven different pairs of glasses, interchanging them at various times. He also had a cheap watch hanging from a piece of cord tied around his waist. All these we copied precisely from the photographs.

Many people remember Gandhi as a little old man dressed in a sheet and carrying a beanpole for a staff. He had four staffs of various shapes and sizes. On the Salt March he carried one different from any he had used on previous occasions. Reporters covering the Salt March never wrote that this was 140 cm long. Only the photographs could give us this detail.

Gandhi had several different spinning wheels, or *charkas,* and he held the thread in a particular way when he spun. We were able to capture these idiosyncrasies while Ben was spinning.

We built from scratch an exact replica of Gandhi's *ashram* at Sabarmati. In reality, it was outside Ahmadabad, but we reconstructed it on the river outside Delhi. Every building, every fence and every cooking pot was recreated from the photographs. We were even lucky enough to have the time to plant and grow crops that were historically accurate.

Photographs even helped with the music for the film. I was at a loss to know how to cope with the beginning of the Salt March until I noticed in a still a marcher carrying a single-stringed Indian instrument.

India's first prime minister, Jawaharlal Nehru, was a close associate of Gandhi's over many years. He was immensely kind to me when I visited him in Delhi in 1963 to request his cooperation in the making of the film. He introduced me to his daughter, Indira Gandhi (no relation to the Mahatma), who later became Prime Minister herself. Mrs. Gandhi has been very supportive to the making of the film, even to the extent of loaning some of her father's clothes so that the tailor in Delhi could copy them for Roshan Seth who plays Pandit Nehru.

We discovered details to help depict all the main characters in the film. Mohammed Ali Jinnah's Saville Row suits, the white streak in his hair, handkerchief in his pocket, ever-present cigarette. The great Indian nationalist Gopal Krishna Gokhale, who was Gandhi's mentor early in his political career—glasses, moustache, tasselled hat, even the way he threw his scarf over his shoulder. Sardar Patel's baldness and the particular shawl he always wore. Lord Louis Mountbatten as he was in his forties when he was the last British Viceroy in India—a full head of dark hair, double-breasted suits with wide lapels and two-tone shoes.

Sequences requiring massive groups of people demanded careful attention to historical detail. Hundreds of thousands of people crowded New Delhi on January 31, 1948, to watch Gandhi's funeral procession. A stunned world followed the event by radio and by newspaper reports and pictures. We assembled a crowd of 200 000 by appealing on radio and television and in newspapers for people to help recreate part of the procession on the thirty-third anniversary of Gandhi's death. We also transported 85 000 villagers into Delhi from the countryside, to which were added servicemen and mourners bringing the total of those present to over 300 000. I had never directed a scene involving such a vast mass of humanity, but the photographs showed us precisely where to place the onlookers along the route of the cortege; which people, including Nehru and Patel, actually stood on the bier; who paced behind it; how to position the military personnel and how we should dress the mourners in the procession.

I shall never forget that day. I was humbled by the same sentiment that Albert Einstein had so eloquently voiced: "Generations to come will scarce believe that such a one as this ever in flesh and blood walked upon this earth."

Director Richard Attenborough (right) *and Ben Kingsley on the set of Gandhi.*

The Life of Gandhi

The great Indian political leader Mohandas Gandhi was born in 1869 in western India. At the age of nineteen, he went to England to study law. After graduating in 1891, Gandhi returned to India and practised law. Two years later he left for South Africa to work as an attorney for a trading company.

The racism and oppression Gandhi met in South Africa led him to fight for the rights of the Indian community, and he soon emerged as their leader. He organized successful protest campaigns by not cooperating with the government's discriminatory laws. This new technique—passive resistance—was later used to great effect in India's struggle for independence.

Gandhi returned to India in 1915 to a hero's welcome. He was dubbed the "Mahatma," or Great Soul, a traditional Indian honorary title by which he became known throughout the world.

The India Gandhi found upon his return suffered under British colonial rule. About one thousand British civil servants controlled hundreds of millions of Indians. There was a growing movement for independence, but a unified effort was hindered by disagreements between India's Hindus and Moslems, and by the caste system which prevented lower castes from having much influence in Indian society.

Gandhi's campaign for Indian self-government included nonviolence, mass non-cooperation, fasting and imprisonment. He became a figure of great moral authority.

One of Gandhi's most effective protests was the Salt March of 1940. In a hot country such as India, salt is a necessity of life, and the colonial law dictated that it had to be bought from the British. Gandhi organized a 385-km march to the ocean where he picked up salt from the shore, openly disobeying the British law.

On August 14, 1947 India became an independent country. Gandhi had wanted Hindus and Moslems to live together in one united country, but disagreements continued and a separate Moslem country, Pakistan, was created. Gandhi continued his work for unity, starting a fast for peace among India's warring communities. His pleas for co-operation angered some and on January 30, 1948, Gandhi was assassinated by one of his own countrymen.

There are differing views about Gandhi's personality and methods. Perhaps his most important contribution to India's struggle for independence was his spiritual leadership and influence.

Responding

1. How do you know that Gandhi was one of the most influential leaders of all time?
2. Do you think that Attenborough's acting background contributed to the greatness of the movie *Gandhi?* Why or why not?
3. Why do you think the actors gained confidence from looking at historical photographs of Gandhi and his times?

FOCUS ON THE CREATIVE PROCESS

Directing a Movie

Go over what you learned about the director's role in making a movie from Attenborough's article:

- the long planning stage,
- working with actors,
- attention to visual detail,
- choosing settings and music.

Which do you think are the three most important qualities of a film director? Defend your choices with reference to the article.

Extending

1. Obtain a video of *Gandhi* and watch it with a partner. What difference, if any, did Attenborough's article make to your perception of the movie?
2. Research the life of Gandhi to learn why he became such an important figure in the Indian struggle for independence from British rule.

DREAMING A MYTH OF CREATION

Jessica Pegis

I t took four years to bring *In the Land of the Spirits* to its world premiere in Ottawa on November 16, 1988—four years of planning, fund-raising, composing, choreographing, designing and rehearsing. Still, that was very little time compared with the centuries of tradition that made this work possible.

In the Land of the Spirits is the first Native ballet to have been written, produced and performed by Native people. It was developed by composer Miklos Massey and conductor John Kim Bell, a Mohawk and founder of the Canadian Native Arts Foundation (CNAF). Bell says he hoped the production would stimulate interest in Native culture and mythology and encourage Native children and adolescents to pursue a career in the arts. He says that while "the arts haven't been a big part of Native life, neither has playing hockey or being a civil servant. I think it's a matter of time, money and offering the kids the right opportunities."

One reason why *In the Land of the Spirits* is the perfect vehicle for Native talent is that it combines the old and the new—an Ojibway creation myth and a modern story about conquering alcohol abuse. The ballet opens with the descent to earth of Winona, the first woman, who is united with the Creator. Their union produces a serene Native society that thrives for centuries. Gradually, however, the community discovers it cannot seal itself away from the world. The winds of social change are blowing, brought on by European exploration, and later, the industrial and technological revolutions.

Thousands of years after Winona's descent to earth, a young man (the hero) known simply as "the Alcoholic" notices her picture painted on a mural and falls in love with her. Winona comes to life, believing that the hero is her lost Creator. The two form a friendship, which is interrupted when the jealous Evil Lord of the Underworld takes Winona to his mystical realm, the Land of the Spirits. It is now left to the Alcoholic to save Winona.

Ultimately, the hero not only rescues Winona but saves himself: in one of the pivotal scenes, he smashes the Evil Lord with his only available weapon, an empty liquor bottle. Winona reappears to him, invites him to join her forever in the paradise that was once theirs, but he declines. He is cured of his alcoholism and chooses reality instead—"his own reality," underlines Bell. "The value of this story to me occurs in that scene when Winona beckons the hero to come live with her in the past. He decides not to go. The moral of the story is that we, as Native people, can't go back and live like we did a thousand years ago. Instead, we must go forward with courage and strength."

It turned out that a healthy dose of both was required to plan and mount *In the Land of the Spirits.* Existing ballet companies were reluctant to get involved with the project and some of Bell's friends told him that without money, experience or dancers, he would never pull it off. He was president of CNAF at the time and had only two assistants, Judy Tobe and Shelle Brant, to help with fund-raising and administration. Then Northern Telecom agreed to be a corporate sponsor for the ballet

John Kim Bell, composer, conductor and founder of the Canadian Native Arts Foundation.

and the real work began: searching for native artists to fill the three principal roles—Winona (Suzanne Brown), the Alcoholic (Mark Antonio Lopez), and the Evil Lord of the Underworld (Raoul Trujillo).

"We searched Canada and the United States and found only eight professionally trained native dancers," says Bell. He was not able to find any Native choreographers or people with expertise in set, costume or lighting design, so instead he hired the best people availa-ble who would "respect the story and concept of the production," and paired each one with a Native person who could act as a consultant. He did, however, locate one Sioux artist, Maxine Noel, who collaborated with the nine-time Dora Award winner Mary Kerr, a costume designer. Together they created some of the most dazzling sets and costumes ever showcased in the history of Canadian ballet.

In composing the music for *In the Land of the Spirits,* Bell had something

The Creator gives life to one of his creatures in a scene from "In the Land of the Spirits."

authentic but also "fresh and original" in mind. One stumbling block was that traditional Native music actually sounds like the music featured in all those Hollywood movies. "It was a challenge," says Bell, "not to capture the sound of the Hollywood Western, even though much of that music is authentic. It's usually one voice and a drum, or a flute and a drum. But once you harmonize it, it generates a kind of song, so that's what we did." The original score for *In the Land of the Spirits* was composed by Bell and Miklos Massey and fully orchestrated for an eighty-piece orchestra.

To create the sets and costumes for *In the Land of the Spirits,* Mary Kerr and Maxine Noel decided to meet first to discuss Native dress and ceremony, then retired to their respective studios to work on some preliminary designs. When they met again, they discovered that one element predominated in each other's work: the circle, the symbol of creation—that which has no beginning or end.

The sets for *In the Land of the Spirits* are colourful, dramatic and often whimsical. In the opening scene, a huge tree of life grows out of a tortoise, and animals of the earth who greet Winona are gloriously attired in peacock blue, fuschia, orange, pink and green. In the climactic scene in which the hero has conquered his alcoholism, something close to magic happens: as the hero faces the audience, stretching out his arms in victory, his shadow is transformed into the image of a mighty eagle. At the ballet's premiere at the Ottawa Arts Centre, this scene inspired a ten-minute standing ovation.

In retrospect, Bell says, "when I look at the progress we made, I am still haunted by those who said this was an experimental work that could not succeed." That surely made the over 100 000-dollar profit realized from the Ottawa premiere all the more satisfying. With the proceeds, and with further funds collected by CNAF, Bell has established what he calls "a Canada Council for Native young people"—a fund of grants and scholarships intended for Native youth.

"The drop-out rate among Native high school students is sixty to seventy per cent. That's much higher than the national average. I believe that you've got to give opportunities to kids very early, offer them something they would love to do. Because that's how people learn to like themselves, by accomplishing something."

Asked how much his own background has shaped his present interests, Bell comments that "My mum was a single parent—we didn't have it easy." The family had lived on the Kahnawake reserve near Montreal during Bell's infancy, but his mother took him and his brother to Ohio when Bell was three. He requested piano lessons at the age of eight and was pronounced musically gifted not long after that. Predictably, his talent provoked some interest and jealousy among his peers—"the guys would take a number to beat me up for studying piano!"—but he chuckles about it now.

It only made him more interested in music and more passionate about giving Native talent a chance. After *In the Land of the Spirits,* that's hardly a risky business.

Responding

1. Do you think presentations like *In the Land of the Spirits* stimulate interest in Native culture? Do they encourage Native young people to become involved in the arts?
2. In the ballet, what is the significance of the Alcoholic's refusing to join Winona in paradise?
3. What was ironic about the Native music chosen for the ballet?

FOCUS ON VIEWING AND REPRESENTING

Designing a Set and Theme Music

A stage presentation is in large part a visual experience for the audience. Sometimes the set is so spectacular or attractive that it wins applause even before the actors or performers appear.

Work with a partner to design a set for a live performance.

- Think of an occasion, perhaps a recital, a school variety night, a play or a performance by a band.
- Decide how the shape of the stage will accommodate the movements of the performers, where they will move, what equipment will be in place and so forth.
- Think about the performance itself, the feelings it will arouse and decide on a theme or basic idea for your design. What shapes will you use for the set? What colours will be appropriate?
- Sketch and colour the set. If it is for a real, not imaginary, performance, check it out with the people who will actually use it. Make any modifications you and they feel are appropriate.
- If the performance calls for music, listen to recordings to find something which supports the theme.
- Share your drawings and music selections with other groups of students.

Extending

1. Talk to young artists in music, drama or dance to find out how they got their start. How did their early career compare with that of John Kim Bell?
2. Agencies like the National Film Board have videos and films of Native dances. Arrange for a group of students to view a selection of these.

  - How would you describe the dances?
  - What spiritual and cultural significance do they have?

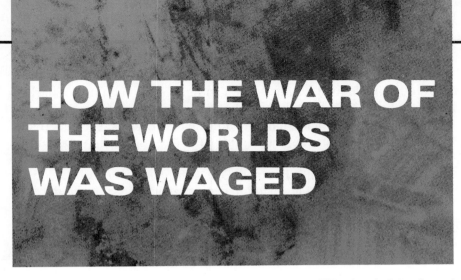

HOW THE WAR OF THE WORLDS WAS WAGED

Elizabeth MacLeod

"We know that in the early years of the twentieth century this world was being watched closely by intelligences greater than man's. . ."

That's how it all began, the famous radio broadcast of the story *The War of the Worlds* that sent Americans into a panic. Orson Welles, the twenty-three-year-old director and star of the show, updated and dramatized a story by the British writer H. G. Wells and, by carefully applying his knowledge of effective radio techniques, he made a show so realistic that listeners were completely drawn into it.

The story begins with reports of gas explosions on Mars, quickly followed by meteorites landing near the little town of Grovers Mill, New Jersey. Those meteorites are soon revealed to be spaceships from Mars, full of monstrous creatures throwing flames and destroying everything in their paths. These hideous aliens march across the northeastern U.S. and take over New York City. The story is continued by the university professor who originally spots those explosions on Mars and is trying to make his way to New York City to discover if there are any humans still alive there. Instead, he finds the Martians, killed by Earth's bacteria, to which earthlings are immune.

Radio Days

There was nothing unusual about the broadcast. Welles had been saving the story as his special "trick" for Hallowe'en, but otherwise this show was part of regular programming, seventeenth in a drama series broadcast on CBS radio by Welles's "Mercury Theatre." Welles was frustrated that his show was on the radio at the same time as the top-rated ventriloquist Edgar Bergen and his wooden dummy Charlie McCarthy, so he set out to create the best show he could.

Welles didn't have a lot of money for the show, so the special effects were simple. For instance, the sound of the alien spaceship opening was made by holding a jar in a toilet bowl (to heighten the echo effect) and unscrewing the lid! What made *The War of the Worlds* so effective were the techniques Welles used to dramatize it. The story begins with dance music supposedly being broadcast from a popular New York club. Suddenly the program is interrupted by the first of many news bulletins telling of the landing of the meteorites. The music is then broken up by explanations of these occurrences and by an on-the-scene reporter. He is describing the advance of this deadly enemy when suddenly his microphone goes dead! (The broadcast is available on tapes and records if you want to hear it for yourself.)

Panic!

"Incredible as it may seem, both the observations of science and the evidence of our eyes lead to the inescapable assumption that those strange beings who landed in the Jersey farmlands tonight are the vanguard of an invading army from the planet Mars..."

Many people think it was this announcement that really caused the panic since people just tuning in thought they were hearing real news dispatches. It was followed by a realistic speech from the "Secretary of the Interior" describing the destruction.

The results were incredible and almost instantaneous. People poured into the streets, rushing to police stations, hospitals, churches—anywhere they thought they could get information or help! Those who lived in cities tried to get into the country and those who lived in the country struggled into the city. Streets and phone lines were jammed as people tried to get to their families and friends to spend their last minutes on earth together. There were reports of fights, heart attacks and hysteria, and some people later claimed that they saw the Martians and the smoke from their attack. Electric companies were inundated with calls asking them to cut the power and cause a blackout so the aliens wouldn't be able to find the cities. Doctors and nurses called hospitals volunteering to help with the wounded, and people stood on street corners hoping to catch a glimpse of any battles.

Some of the reactions now seem funny. One woman called up a bus terminal for information, and when the clerk was slow in helping her, she tried to speed him up by saying "Hurry, please, the world is

Orson Welles delivers his famous 1938 broadcast of "The War of the Worlds" at a New York studio.

coming to an end and I have a lot to do." Police cars in New Jersey were all tuned in to CBS which meant the Chief of Police couldn't get through to any of his officers. He phoned the radio station demanding that Orson Welles instruct the police cars to return to their stations since he couldn't reach them. One man tried to break into a theatre to warn the moviegoers inside of the terrible situation, but the manager wouldn't let him in since he thought the fellow was just trying to sneak into the movie for free. The manager then called the police for verification of the story and so prevented a panicky, dangerous stampede out of the theatre.

Life on Mars?

Why did so many people panic? The main reason is that the broadcast came soon after there had been a war scare in Europe and people were used to having radio shows interrupted for reports on the situation. Another important reason for the panic was that fifty years ago, many people thought that there could be intelligent life on Mars. They thought the canyons or "tracks" on the planet might be canals built by a dying civilization trying to transport dwindling water supplies. If these thirsty Martians were looking for another planet to take over, the neighbouring Earth, which is mostly covered with water, would look very appealing.

Orson Welles was also extremely clever about the way he presented his drama. He knew the weak spot in the Edgar Bergen–Charlie McCarthy show occurred about fifteen minutes into the show when the guest, usually a bad singer, performed. At that point most listeners twiddled with the radio dial to find something better. Welles paced his show so that the announcement which described the broadcast as a dramatization was over long before most people tuned in. Once they started listening, Welles kept them hooked with his brilliant use of documentary techniques and painstaking detail. Because the audience was so involved, very few changed stations to hear other reports on the situation. And when the show ended, few people heard Welles's reassurance that the show had been a hoax—most of the listeners were out in the streets or on the highways fleeing to safety.

Would such a panic happen today? Probably not. Television was not widely available in 1938 and radio has lost much of the importance it had then. Even a similar show broadcast on TV wouldn't have the same impact because we have so many channels from which to choose that there is rarely such a huge number of people watching one show. Also, Orson Welles's show wasn't interrupted by commercials, so the intense mood of the dramatization was sustained throughout. Advertising has also taught us to be more critical of information we get through the media. Nowadays, we're not as likely to accept something as fact without checking it first.

Orson Welles never admitted whether he intended to cause such a sensation. In fact, he said he had hesitated to present the show because he was worried that "People might be bored or annoyed at hearing a tale so improbable." However, because of the broadcast, he was able to raise the money to write, direct and star in *Citizen Kane,* a movie many people consider one of the best ever.

Today there is a statue in Grovers Mills, New Jersey (there really is such a place!), commemorating *The War of the Worlds* broadcast. It shows Welles at a microphone, a family glued to its radio and an alien spacecraft lurking near by.

Responding

1. Does the reaction to the broadcast strike you as funny or sad? Why?
2. What do you think were the motives of the town councillors who erected a statue commemorating *The War of the Worlds?*
3. Have you ever been fooled by a radio or television show? What happened?

FOCUS ON DRAMA AND THE MEDIA

Plausibility

Choose a play you have read which could be adapted to a radio play. "Frankenstein," in the *In Context Two* anthology, is a radio play and would work well for this task.

With a partner, decide how you would direct the play to make it seem plausible to a radio audience.

Consider how you would handle each of the following:

- *Casting the characters so that they would play their parts convincingly.* What qualities would you look for when people audition for the parts?
- *Adapting or rewriting the script to fit current events. (The War of the Worlds* succeeded because it referred to what was happening around the time of the broadcast.) Refer to things your audience is familiar with.
- *Use of sound effects.* These don't need to be over-used so they overwhelm the story, but they are necessary to prevent the dramatization from sounding like a reading.
- *A realistic dramatization.* Play down the things that might make the audience skeptical. Play up the things the audience will feel familiar with.

When your decisions are made, meet with another group to exchange ideas.

Extending

1. Listen to a recording of *The War of the Worlds.* Can you understand why people were so convinced it was real? What does the experience teach you about the times when it was broadcast?
2. Orson Welles wouldn't reveal whether he had intended to fool people with *The War of the Worlds.* What do you think? Was it an accident? Do you think people could be fooled in a similar way with a television show today? Why or why not?

SO YOU WANT TO BE AN ACTOR...

Jeff Siamon

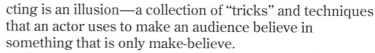
cting is an illusion—a collection of "tricks" and techniques that an actor uses to make an audience believe in something that is only make-believe.

The actor slowly moves across the stage, her cheeks wet with tears. She slumps into a chair. Her world has been shattered. Her hopes and dreams destroyed.

Only five metres away, the audience shares her pain. Their eyes are damp. They have the same feeling of despair. They, too, sit slumped in their seats.

Even though the audience knows that they are sitting in a theatre and *not* in someone's living room, the skill of the actor makes this moment real. But how does she do it? How can she portray a character different from her own? How does she create the illusion of a character?

If you were an actor, how would you create this illusion?

Who Am I...?

Think about the person you're going to play. What's that person like? Why does that person act the way he or she does? What makes your character different from the other characters in the play or script? From yourself?

Actors try to answer these and other questions about the roles they play. Before rehearsal begins, they often develop a character profile—an imaginary history of the person they are playing. Can you answer these questions about the character you are playing?

Lucy Peacock as Eliza in My Fair Lady (top), *and as Nora in* A Doll's House (bottom).

My Character's Background

- When was I born?
- What was it like growing up in my family?
- What were my friends like? My enemies? Who are my friends now? Enemies?
- What were my favourite toys? (Pastimes? Food? etc.)
- What type of person am I? (Shy? Aggressive? Social? Lonely? etc.)
- What problems or conflicts do I have? Goals? Ambitions?
- What makes me feel good? Bad?
- *What other questions can you think of?*

If all this seems like a lot of work just to prepare for a part, it is. Actors work very hard even before they read a line or step out on to a stage.

Of course, preparing yourself for your role is only the beginning. An audience needs more than this. They need to *hear* and *see* the character.

Speak the Speech...

In modern theatre, film and television, characters speak naturally, the way you and your friends do. This was not always the case, however. Actors would often "strut" across the stage, strike an exaggerated pose and deliver their lines in an overly dramatic way. Audiences today probably wouldn't accept those artificial conventions of dramatic speech.

But speaking in front of people is not as easy as it looks. Acting, after all, isn't *real* life. Without special training, an actor's voice can easily get lost in a theatre or seem muffled when recorded on tape or film.

In fact, much of the dramatic speech that actors use *is* exaggerated and unnatural. But it is their skill and voice training which gives an audience the illusion of natural speech.

Think about how you pronounce certain words: children, government, newspaper. Most people say *chooldr'n, gov'rment, noospapa.* In normal speech, sounds difficult to pronounce are either omitted or changed. This is okay if you are talking directly to someone, but try standing back twenty or thirty metres. Few people will be able to understand you.

Proper voice training, like learning to play an instrument, takes years to perfect. The voice exercises that actors practise help them to pronounce words distinctly yet quickly.

Try some of these "tongue twisters." Speak slowly at first, then gradually speed up. Be sure to pronounce *all* the correct sounds.

Lucy Peacock plays Ophelia, the distressed heroine of Hamlet.

Without a great deal of practice (and that's something actors do a lot— practise), you will find these exercises difficult, especially if you talk quickly. Can you be understood twenty metres away? An actor can.

- Peak, pick, peck, pack, puck, perk, park, pock, pork, poke, pike.
- Judge not that ye be not judged, for with what judgement ye judge ye shall be judged.
- The sea ceaseth and sufficeth us.
- The very merry Mary crossed the ferry in a furry coat.
- The weary wanderer wondered wistfully whether winsome Winifred would weep.

Naturally, there is more to speech training than "tongue twisters." You will need to learn how to breathe correctly, so that your voice won't get tired and hoarse. You will have to practise "projecting," so that you can be heard without sounding loud or forced. And you will need to know about and be able to imitate the qualities of speech which make up different dialects and speech patterns.

My Kingdom for a Hat...

Just as speech helps create the actor's illusion, costume allows actors another way to develop their characters.

Have you ever watched children playing with "dress-ups"? Someone puts on a large, floppy hat and suddenly they are transformed. They act differently. They move differently. They feel differently. So actors are transformed by the costumes their characters wear. Actors have not lost the childlike ability to pretend to be someone else.

Notice the two characters in the photographs. Both are played by the same actress, yet because of costume (and, of course, make-up) each seems like a totally different person.

Clothes in general tell an audience a great deal about a character. Movie actors in particular have often used costume as a kind of trademark, something which identifies their screen characters.

Think about the character you are playing. Is there any special clothing which is individual to that character? A hat? A pair of shoes? Glasses? In rehearsing your role, wear something that the character likes. Try changing your character's costume during rehearsal. How does each new costume you wear affect the way you (the character) feel? Does it change the way the character speaks or moves? Let your costume stimulate your actor's imagination.

All the Right Moves. . .

A man walks into a crowded room—a wedding reception. He accidentally spills a plate of sandwiches. He trips and falls on top of the wedding cake. He steps on his partner's feet while dancing. Are these the actions of a successful politician? The president of a large corporation? A famous dancer with the National Ballet? Probably not.

How an actor moves—or how the *character* he or she is portraying moves—also helps create the illusion.

Have you ever recognized someone from far off, too far to actually see the face? How do you do it? Actually, what you are recognizing is the way that person moves. Like a signature, movement is distinct and individual. Actors understand this. Much of their training teaches them how to control the muscles of their body so that they can imitate the way people move.

Shake hands with a friend. Now shake hands again, but this time pretend to be a concert pianist. A professional athlete. A labourer. A child. A very old person. Someone who is shy. Aggressive. Absent-minded. Unhappy. Excited. Now try it again, only this time shake hands with an *enemy.*

If you consider that the characters actors play not only shake hands, but walk, sit, stare, "slump"—move in a variety of ways—you can imagine how many elements actors must consider when using movement to develop their characters.

Here is one exercise actors use when trying to explore the way their characters move. With another actor and a small audience, rehearse a scene *without* speaking any lines. Use movement and expression to communicate the missing dialogue.

Can the audience understand you? Your fellow actor? After your scene, think about those elements of movement which were successful, which conveyed the emotions and thoughts you felt. Consider incorporating them when you next speak your lines.

The illusion is complete if the actor has been able to move or amuse an audience. For that one special moment in a darkened theatre, make-believe is something both actor and audience believe in.

Responding

1. Do you like acting in plays? Why or why not?
2. If you took the advice in the article, do you think you would find acting easier and become a better actor? What makes you think so?
3. Why do you think people "act differently" when they put on a costume and makeup?

Preparing a Role

Actors use a variety of exercises and techniques to "get inside" a character they are preparing to play. Choose a role you would be interested in playing in a play you have enjoyed and try the following techniques.

1. Write an autobiographical sketch of the person you will be playing. Pick a time in the character's past such as

   - a summer holiday,
   - a moment of triumph or defeat,
   - an important turning point in personal or professional life.

     Write as if the character were speaking. Don't worry about grammar or spelling. Just let the character's thoughts flow.
2. Imagine you are looking at a photograph of the character. Either describe the photo to other actors or record your thoughts on tape. Try to answer these questions in your description.

   - Who besides yourself is in the photo?
   - Where was it taken?
   - What's in the background? The foreground?
   - What were you thinking the moment the shutter was snapped?
   - What happened just before the photo? After?
   - How did you feel then?
   - How do you feel now looking at the picture?

Extending

1. Get together with a group of other students and try out some of the ideas in the article.

   - shaking hands with different kinds of people
   - rehearsing a scene without lines
   - working with tongue twisters

     Did the methods start you thinking creatively about what you're doing with your part?
2. Research the method of voice coaches. Contact the Drama Department of a university or a community drama instructor for information about the techniques.